Mastering the Art of Gratitude

A journey from acknowledgement to awakening.

VOLUME II

"Gratitude is not what you feel — it's how your soul learns to see."

SHREE SHAMBAV

Mastering the Art of Gratitude
A journey from acknowledgement to awakening.
Volume II

Shree Shambav

Published by Shree Shambav, Tamil Nadu, India
Shree Shambav Ink & Imagination "Where Words Breathe and Imagination Soars"

First Edition, 2026

ISBN: 978-93-5635-011-3
Email:shreeshambav@gmail.com
Web:www.shambav.org

DEDICATION

"Isavasyam idam sarvam yat kim ca jagatyam jagat, tena tyaktena bhunjitha, ma gridhah kasyasvid dhanam"

To the Almighty,

the Divine Masters,

the family who listens,

and my parents who see –

your presence shapes the pages of my life's journey.

"Isavasyam idam sarvam yat kim ca jagatyam jagat"

Meaning: "God encompasses everything you perceive, see, or touch with your sense organs."

DISCLAIMER

Mastering the Art of Gratitude: A Journey from Acknowledgement to Awakening is a personal exploration and reflection on the transformative power of gratitude. This book arises from the author's sincere intention to understand, embody, and share the deeper dimensions of appreciation as a path toward inner awakening.

The content within these pages is intended solely for personal enrichment, contemplation, and educational purposes. It represents the author's experiences, insights, and interpretations of spiritual and psychological principles, and is not offered as professional advice, therapy, or a substitute for qualified guidance. Readers are encouraged not to use the material for clinical, diagnostic, financial, legal, or therapeutic purposes.

While every effort has been made to ensure authenticity and depth of reflection, the author makes no warranties or representations regarding the completeness, applicability, or accuracy of the content. By reading this book, you acknowledge that the author shall not be held responsible for any loss, discomfort, or consequence—direct or indirect—arising from the interpretation or use of the material presented.

The teachings of gratitude, mindfulness, and presence can evoke emotional awareness and personal introspection. Any such experiences are a natural part of inner exploration and are meant to encourage reflection, not distress. Readers are invited to approach the material with openness, discernment, and self-compassion.

This book does not seek to impose beliefs or practices but to invite readers into a conscious dialogue with life itself. It is a humble offering—an invitation to rediscover the grace hidden in everyday moments, to see beauty in imperfection, and to awaken the heart's quiet knowing.

Ultimately, *Mastering the Art of Gratitude* is shared in the spirit of love, reverence, and illumination. The reader alone is responsible for interpreting and integrating its ideas in ways that align with their personal truth and inner journey.

Note: For knowledge purpose only.

Note - If any part of the book, in any sequence, hurts the reader's sentiments, it would be just out of a sheer accident not intentional

EPIGRAPH

Gratitude is more than thought; it is vibration. It turns resistance into flow, scarcity into abundance, and the mundane into sacred. When the heart aligns with appreciation, life itself becomes a mirror reflecting love, presence, and infinite possibility.

– Shree Shambav

Mastering the Art of Gratitude

A journey from acknowledgement to awakening.

"Gratitude is not what you feel — it's how your soul learns to see."

SHREE SHAMBAV
Shree Shambav is a 108x best-selling author, renowned for his transformative works in personal development and spiritual growth

Dear Cherished Readers

Dear Cherished Readers,

As I embark on this new literary voyage, my heart swells with profound gratitude and an overwhelming sense of connection. With deep emotion, I extend my heartfelt appreciation to each of you who has joined me on this journey.

With sincere warmth, I invite you to revisit the steps we have taken together through the pages of my earlier works. Our odyssey began with "Journey of Soul - Karma," a book that marked my first foray into the world of words and a testament to the raw passion that ignited my writing adventure.

The subsequent chapters of our shared journey unfolded through the enchanting tapestry of the *"Twenty + One"* series. With each page turned, it felt as though a brushstroke was added to the canvas of our collective imagination—stories and sentiments woven to echo within the quiet corners of your heart. These weren't just words; they were invitations to feel, to reflect, and to remember what truly matters.

And how can I not cherish the transformative path we walked together through the *"Life Changing Journey—Inspirational Quotes Series?"* Day by day, quote by quote, we ventured inward—into spaces often overlooked—to find wisdom in simplicity and light in life's shadows. Each reflection was offered as a gentle whisper of hope, a spark meant to uplift, inspire, and remind us that even in silence, the soul speaks.

The release of "Death - Light of Life and the Shadow of Death" promises to shed new light on the timeless mystery of death.

The **Optimum Python Series** is a comprehensive learning pathway designed to empower readers at every stage of their programming journey. It begins with **Series I: Ultimate Guide for Beginners**, which builds a strong and accessible foundation in Python for newcomers. **Series II: Exploring Data Structures and Algorithms** advances into core computer science concepts, strengthening problem-solving skills and coding efficiency.

Building on this, **Series III: Python Power for Data Science** introduces powerful libraries such as NumPy, Pandas, Matplotlib, and Scikit-learn, guiding readers through data manipulation, visualisation, and foundational machine learning techniques. **Series IV: Unleashing the Potential of Data Science with Machine Learning Techniques** explores advanced models and real-world applications.

This progression continues with **Series V: Optimum: Python Power – Unleashing the Potential of Data Science with Deep Learning Techniques**, and culminates in **Series VI: From Data to Intelligence – The Deep Learning Revolution**, enabling readers to harness the full potential of data-driven innovation. Whether you are a beginner or an advanced learner, this series serves as your complete roadmap to Python mastery and beyond.

Shree Shambav expands his artistic repertoire with *Whispers of Eternity: A Symphony of Soulful Verses*, a heartfelt exploration of the human experience expressed through lyrical depth and timeless reflection. Complementing this, his *Whispers of the Soul: A Journey Through Haiku* distils profound truths into delicate, poignant verses, capturing the fleeting essence of life with elegant simplicity.

Equally evocative, *Whispers of Stillness: Where the Soul Listens Beyond the Noise* offers meditative couplets that invite readers into silence, where wisdom blossoms in the spaces between words. Together, these works illuminate Shambav's versatility and mastery of soulful expression. They invite readers on a transformative journey of self-discovery, weaving a tapestry of emotion, insight, and transcendence that lingers long after the final page is turned.

Building on this success, he continued to enchant audiences with his subsequent albums: HeartStrings, *Melodies of the Heart, Driftwood Memories, Winds of Change, The Veil and the Waves, Echoes of the Soul, Phoenix Within,* Uncaged, Where Nature Sings and Wings of Forever. Each album further solidified his place in the world of music, offering a mesmerising collection of tracks that evoke nostalgia, introspection, and heartfelt connection. With every composition, Shree Shambav weaves a musical journey that lingers in the soul long after the final note fades.

Shree Shambav's latest works shine as luminous beacons on the path of self-discovery, mindful living, and spiritual awakening. His writings span a vast spectrum of human experience, each book offering a doorway to transformation. Among his most celebrated titles are Learn to Love Yourself: A Journey of Discovering Inner Beauty and Strength Through 10 Transformative Rules, The Power of Letting Go: Embrace Freedom and Happiness, A Journey of Lasting Peace, and The Entitlement Trap: Get Over It, Get On.

His thought-provoking works include Whispers of a Dying Soul: Unspoken Regrets and Unlived Dreams, Whispers of Silence: Unlocking Inner Power through

Stillness, The Power of Words: Transforming Speech, Transforming Lives, The Art of Intentional Living: Minimalism for a Life of Purpose, and Awakening the Infinite: The Power of Consciousness in Transforming Life.

In The Power of Manifestation: Unlocking the Path from Thought to Reality, Shree Shambav offers a transformative roadmap for turning vision into reality, while Beyond the Veil: A Journey Through Life After Death explores the profound mystery of what lies beyond earthly existence. His other powerful works include Bonds Beyond Blood: Where Love Builds Bridges and Bonds Defy Blood, a celebration of love that transcends lineage, The Inner Battlefield: Overcoming the Enemies of the Mind and Soul, a guide to conquering inner conflicts, and A Journey into Spiritual Maturity: 12 Golden Rules for Inner Transformation, which offers timeless wisdom for the evolving seeker. In The Seeker's Gold: Unlocking Life's Greatest Treasure, he inspires readers to discover the hidden riches of the soul, while The Law of Attraction: A Soulful Path reveals how to harmonise thought, energy, and intention to create a life aligned with one's highest purpose. His transformative Born to Rise series further empowers readers to embrace growth, clarity, and lasting fulfilment.

In addition to these works, Shree Shambav has recently ventured into astrology with the release of

Astrology Unveiled – Foundations of Ancient Wisdom Series I to XVIII, expanding into the realm of metaphysics. These books explore the foundational principles of Vedic astrology, offering readers a rich and practical understanding of this ancient wisdom.

Your unwavering support, enthusiasm to immerse yourself in my writings, and readiness to embark on these journeys with me have been my greatest sources of inspiration. Your input has been a beacon guiding me through the creation process, moulding these stories into containers of passion, emotion, knowledge, and resonance.

As I unveil this new narrative before you, know that your presence, insights, and shared moments have been my companions. The path we have walked together is etched in the annals of my creative evolution, and it's an honour beyond words to have you by my side once more.

Here's to the readers who have illuminated my path with their presence, who have embraced my stories with open hearts, and who have woven themselves into the very fabric of my literary world. Our journey has been a symbiotic dance of writer and reader, a harmony of souls brought together by the magic of storytelling.

With a heart brimming with appreciation and eyes glistening with anticipation, I extend my deepest gratitude for your unwavering support. Thank you for the memories, the shared emotions, and the countless hours spent in the worlds we've crafted together. As we step into this new adventure, let's continue to explore, feel, and discover the boundless horizons that words can unveil.

Warmly,

Shree Shambav

Suggested Reads

FROM BEST-SELLING AUTHOR

ENDORSEMENTS

"Mastering the Art of Gratitude, Volume II, is a luminous guide for anyone seeking to deepen their connection to life. With profound insight, heartfelt stories, and practical wisdom, it illuminates the subtle currents that shape our perceptions, emotions, and relationships. Each chapter gently teaches how to transform resistance into presence, scarcity into abundance, and ordinary moments into sacred encounters. This book is not just read—it is lived, experienced, and felt, leaving a lasting imprint on the heart and soul."

— Akshaya

About the Author

Shree Shambav is an internationally acclaimed best-selling author, inspirational speaker, artist, philanthropist, life coach, strategist and entrepreneur. A world record holder, his deep passion for music led him to create soul-stirring albums, drawing inspiration from his celebrated poetry collection, Whispers of Eternity. His profound insights have sparked deep personal transformations, guiding countless individuals toward self-discovery, purposeful living, and authenticity.

With an extraordinary ability to unlock human potential, Shree empowers individuals to break through limitations and embrace their highest selves. His writings, lectures, and compassionate guidance continue to uplift lives, fostering resilience, mindfulness, and personal growth.

Shree Shambav is a 108x best-selling author celebrated for his profound contributions to personal development and spiritual growth.

Shree Shambav's literary journey took flight with the celebrated Journey of Soul - Karma, where he delved into the depths of human experience to unveil profound insights. Garnering recognition through multiple literature awards, his repertoire includes esteemed works, such as the Twenty + One Series, and the enlightening Life Changing Journey – Inspirational Quotes series.

As a distinguished alumnus of the Indian Institute of Management and the National Institute of Technology, Shree Shambav brings a wealth of corporate acumen from his tenure in multinational corporations. His most recent publications, including Unveiling the Enigma, Death - Light of Life and the Shadow of Death and Optimum – Power Python Series I, Series II, Series III and Series IV, demonstrate his mastery of both the literary and technical spheres.

Shree Shambav expands his artistic repertoire with *Whispers of Eternity: A Symphony of Soulful Verses*, a heartfelt exploration of the human experience expressed through lyrical depth and timeless reflection. Complementing this, his *Whispers of the Soul: A Journey Through Haiku* distils profound truths into delicate, poignant verses, capturing the fleeting essence of life with elegant simplicity.

Equally evocative, *Whispers of Stillness: Where the Soul Listens Beyond the Noise* offers meditative couplets that invite readers into silence, where wisdom blossoms in the spaces between words. Together, these works illuminate Shambav's versatility and mastery of soulful expression. They invite readers on a transformative journey of self-discovery, weaving a tapestry of emotion, insight, and transcendence that lingers long after the final page is turned.

Building on this success, he continued to enchant audiences with his subsequent albums: HeartStrings, *Melodies of the Heart*, *Driftwood Memories*, *Winds of Change, The Veil and the Waves, Echoes of the Soul, Phoenix Within,* Uncaged, Where Nature Sings and Wings of Forever. Each album further solidified his place in the world of music, offering a mesmerising collection of tracks that evoke nostalgia, introspection, and heartfelt connection. With every composition, Shree Shambav weaves a musical journey that lingers in the soul long after the final note fades.

Shree Shambav's latest works shine as luminous beacons on the path of self-discovery, mindful living, and spiritual awakening. His writings span a vast spectrum of human experience, each book offering a doorway to transformation. Among his most celebrated titles are Learn to Love Yourself: A Journey of Discovering Inner Beauty and Strength Through 10 Transformative Rules, The Power of Letting Go: Embrace Freedom and Happiness, A Journey of Lasting Peace, and The Entitlement Trap: Get Over It, Get On.

His thought-provoking works include Whispers of a Dying Soul: Unspoken Regrets and Unlived Dreams, Whispers of Silence: Unlocking Inner Power through Stillness, The Power of Words: Transforming Speech, Transforming Lives, The Art of Intentional Living: Minimalism for a Life of Purpose, and Awakening the Infinite: The Power of Consciousness in Transforming Life.

In The Power of Manifestation: Unlocking the Path from Thought to Reality, Shree Shambav presents a transformative roadmap for turning vision into lived experience, guiding readers from intention to realisation. Beyond the Veil: A Journey Through Life After Death ventures into the profound mystery of existence beyond the physical realm, inviting contemplation on life, transition, and the eternal soul.

His other compelling works include Bonds Beyond Blood: Where Love Builds Bridges and Bonds Defy Lineage, a heartfelt celebration of love that transcends ancestry and form; The Inner Battlefield: Overcoming the Enemies of the Mind and Soul, a powerful guide to mastering inner conflicts and reclaiming mental sovereignty; and A Journey into Spiritual Maturity: 12 Golden Rules for Inner Transformation, which offers timeless wisdom for seekers evolving toward self-mastery and inner awakening.

In The Seeker's Gold: Unlocking Life's Greatest Treasure, he inspires readers to uncover the hidden riches of the soul, while The Law of Attraction: A Soulful Path reveals how to harmonise thought, energy, and intention to create a life aligned with one's highest purpose. His transformative Born to Rise series further empowers readers to embrace growth, clarity, and lasting fulfilment across every dimension of life.

Shree Shambav is also the author of Mastering the Art of Gratitude: A Journey from Acknowledgment to Awakening, a contemplative series on conscious appreciation, and Whispers of a Silent Monk: Poetic Tales of Love, Loss, and Liberation, a lyrical exploration of silence, surrender, and inner freedom.

In addition, his works Journey of the Soul – Karma Unveiled, Unveiling the Enigma, and Death: Light of

Life and the Shadow of Death have been translated into Gujarati and Hindi, extending his spiritual insights to a wider audience.

In addition to these works, Shree Shambav has recently ventured into astrology with the release of Astrology Unveiled – Foundations of Ancient Wisdom Series I to XVII, expanding into the realm of metaphysics. These books explore the foundational principles of Vedic astrology, offering readers a rich and practical understanding of this ancient wisdom.

Shree Shambav established the Ayur Rakshita Foundation, which is dedicated to promoting boundless growth, universal fraternity, and environmental protection. The charity helps diverse communities while working for societal progress.

To learn more about Shree Shambav and his works, visit his website at www.shambav.org. For information about the Ayur Rakshita Foundation and its initiatives, visit www.shambav-ayurrakshita.org.

Let's Follow him on Social Media: **@shreeshambav**

Main: https://linktr.ee/shreeshambav

Website: https://www.shambav.org/

LinkedIn: https://www.linkedin.com/in/shreeshambav/

Blog: https://blog.shambav.org/

Instagram: https://www.instagram.com/shreeshambav/

YouTube: https://www.youtube.com/@shreeshambav

Amazon: https://www.amazon.com/author/shreeshambav

Goodreads: https://www.goodreads.com/author/show/22367436.Shree_Shambav

PREFACE

The Sacred Practice of Remembering

There are moments in life when silence becomes the greatest teacher. When, after all the seeking, striving, and questioning, one simply pauses — and in that pause, something within whispers, *"Thank you."*

That whisper is the beginning of transformation.

This book was born from such pauses — from the quiet moments between breaths, between days, between endings and beginnings — where gratitude reveals itself not as a fleeting feeling, but as a way of seeing. For years, I had spoken and written about gratitude as a principle, a mindset, a key to peace. Yet, it wasn't until I began to *live* it, through both joy and sorrow, that I realised: gratitude is not about what we have; it is about *how we hold life itself.*

Volume I introduced the foundations of gratitude — its psychology, its philosophy, and its emotional practice. It helped us recognise the power of appreciation in healing, presence, and purpose. But this second volume — *A Journey from Acknowledgement to Awakening* — invites us deeper. It explores the *alchemy* of gratitude: how it transforms energy, perception, and consciousness itself.

Gratitude begins as acknowledgement — a thankfulness for blessings received. But through awareness and practice, it matures into awakening — a realisation that *everything*, even pain, is part of life's grace. Between these two states lies the essence of this book: the journey from surface emotion to soul vibration, from noticing beauty to *becoming* it.

This volume unfolds in two parts.

Part One – The Heart of Belonging explores gratitude as the bridge between hearts. In relationships, it becomes empathy. In nature, reverence. In daily practice, it becomes rhythm — the pulse of mindful living. Gratitude here is not an act but a presence, a way of walking gently through the world, recognising divinity in the familiar.

Part Two – The Alchemy of Gratitude moves beyond emotion into energy — into the subtle science of vibration. It unveils how thoughts, emotions, and intentions carry frequencies that shape the quality of our lives. Gratitude, in this light, becomes a tuning fork for the soul — harmonising the mind, body, and spirit with the greater flow of existence.

Throughout these chapters, you will find dialogues between Guruji and his devotees — moments of inquiry, reflection, and revelation. You will meet characters who question, resist, and ultimately rediscover themselves through gratitude. Each conversation is not merely a teaching but a mirror — inviting you to see your own patterns of resistance, scarcity, and awakening reflected within.

Stories like *"The Stone and the Stream"* or *"The Gardener and the Seeds"* are not parables meant to instruct, but pathways meant to remind — that wisdom often hides in simplicity, and the deepest truths arrive softly, like dawn after a long night.

This book is not written to teach gratitude as a concept. It is written to *evoke* it — to help you feel the texture of appreciation in your breath, your relationships, and your inner dialogue. To remind you that even in moments of loss or uncertainty, there remains something to bow to — the silent intelligence guiding it all.

As you read, let these words not be taken as philosophy but as practice. Pause often. Reflect. Observe your heart. For gratitude is not learned through reading; it is awakened by remembering. The purpose of this book is not to fill you with information, but to empty you of forgetfulness — to bring you home to what you have always known but rarely stopped to feel.

When you finish these pages, my wish is not that you understand gratitude better, but that you *live* it more deeply — in the way you greet the morning light, forgive an old wound, or share a smile with a stranger.

Gratitude is the art of remembering that *life itself is a gift* — and that every breath, every tear, every act of love is part of the same sacred whole.

May this book serve as your gentle companion on that journey — from acknowledgement to awakening, from seeking to seeing, from the noise of longing to the stillness of grace.

With kindest regards,

Shree Shambav

CONTENTS

INTRODUCTION

The Journey from Acknowledgement to Awakening

Gratitude is not merely an emotion; it is a way of seeing, a way of being — a lens through which life's fragments reveal their hidden wholeness. To master gratitude is to rediscover the sacred that quietly breathes beneath the ordinary — in the warmth of morning light, in the sound of footsteps returning home, in the unseen kindness of a stranger, or even in the silence that follows loss. Gratitude does not deny pain or pretend perfection; it awakens us to life's deeper rhythm — where every joy, every sorrow, and every pause becomes part of one continuous symphony of meaning.

This second volume, *The Heart of Belonging* and *The Alchemy of Gratitude*, continues the journey begun in the first — moving from the *awareness* of gratitude toward its *embodiment.* If the first volume was about learning to notice life's gifts, this one is about learning to *live* them — to transform acknowledgement into awakening. Gratitude here becomes less about counting blessings and more about *becoming* the blessing.

The world often teaches us to measure life by what is missing. We are conditioned to seek, to strive, to compare. In this chase, we lose touch with the still centre from which appreciation naturally arises. The heart forgets its native language — the quiet "thank you" whispered not out of obligation, but from the recognition that every breath is borrowed light. This book invites the reader to return to that language.

Through stories, dialogues, meditative reflections, and practical guidance, *Mastering the Art of Gratitude* bridges the inner and outer worlds — showing that gratitude is not an act of emotion alone, but of energy, consciousness, and alignment. Each chapter is an unfolding — a movement from mind to heart, from scarcity to sufficiency, from seeking to seeing.

In **Part One: The Heart of Belonging**, gratitude is explored as a living thread weaving through human connection, nature, and daily living. Relationships become sacred mirrors where gratitude deepens through empathy and forgiveness. Nature becomes the first teacher, offering silent lessons in patience, balance, and abundance. And through daily practice, gratitude becomes a rhythm — an inner ritual that sustains emotional harmony and spiritual clarity.

In **Part Two: The Alchemy of Gratitude**, the journey turns inward — toward the shadows that obscure appreciation and the vibrations that sustain it. The reader is invited to meet resistance, scarcity, and emotional pain not as enemies but as invitations. Gratitude, when understood as energy, reveals how every thought and feeling emits a frequency that shapes reality. As the heart begins to align with this understanding, gratitude becomes effortless — not something to be practised, but something to be *remembered.*

This book is not a manual but a mirror — reflecting back the truth that gratitude is already present within you, waiting to be uncovered. The more deeply you listen, the more you realise that gratitude is not a response to life being perfect; it is what makes life sacred, even in its imperfections.

When you pause to thank — not as duty, but as recognition — the world subtly shifts. Relationships soften. The air feels lighter. The mind becomes clear. You begin to see that gratitude is not just a feeling in the heart; it is the frequency of the soul — a vibration that harmonises you with life's infinite intelligence.

Each chapter, reflection, and story in this volume is a step toward that realisation. It is a journey from the mind that seeks to the heart that knows. From acknowledgement — "I have been given" — to awakening — "I have always been whole."

In the quiet spaces between these pages, may you rediscover the music of appreciation — the unseen current that carries all creation. And as you walk through the lessons and practices ahead, may gratitude no longer remain something you express, but something you *are*.

For in the end, the art of gratitude is not learned — it is remembered. It is the soul's return to its original harmony with life.

Warm regards,

Shree Shambav

PROLOGUE

The Temple of Stillness

There are places in the world where silence speaks louder than sound — where the air itself seems to remember prayers whispered centuries ago. Kanchipuram is one such place. Beneath its golden dawns and the lingering fragrance of temple lamps, life moves not in haste but in reverence. It was here, amidst the rustle of sacred fig leaves and the echo of distant chants, that the seed of this book was sown — not in a classroom of thought, but in the living temple of awareness.

There is a force that breathes quietly beneath all our striving — the pulse that unites every joy and sorrow, every meeting and farewell. It is neither loud nor insistent. It waits in stillness, like a river beneath stone, waiting for the heart to listen. That force is **Gratitude** — not as sentiment, but as remembrance.

In a world intoxicated by motion, we often mistake busyness for meaning. We rush through moments meant to be lived slowly. We chase success while forgetting the sacred art of simply *being*. Yet gratitude invites us to pause — to notice the tenderness of sunlight on an old wall, the unspoken kindness in another's eyes, the miracle of breath that arrives unasked, unearned. It reminds us that the divine is not distant; it is present, disguised as the ordinary.

Gratitude is not about collecting reasons to be thankful. It is about dissolving the illusion of lack. It does not demand that life be perfect before we bow in appreciation. It whispers that perfection was never the goal — presence was. For even pain, when held with awareness, becomes a portal to depth. Every ending becomes a teacher. Every challenge, a mirror revealing where grace wishes to enter.

This book, *Mastering the Art of Gratitude – Volume II*, continues where the first left off — but not forward, rather deeper. It is not a manual to be studied, but a mirror to be looked into. Each chapter is a quiet unfolding, guiding the reader from acknowledgement to awakening; from the surface ripples of thankfulness to the still waters of pure being.

Here, relationships become sanctuaries of reflection — teaching us to see others not through expectation, but through compassion. Nature becomes scripture, written in wind and rain, showing us the law of harmony that governs all life. And the unseen forces within — our thoughts, emotions, and vibrations —

are revealed as instruments shaping the music of our reality.

Gratitude, when lived, transforms perception. It turns the mundane into miraculous. The simple act of eating, walking, or breathing becomes a prayer in motion. The silence between words becomes a hymn of belonging. Slowly, we begin to see that gratitude is not what we *do* — it is what we *are* when the noise of separation quiets.

Kanchipuram taught this truth in its own way — not through doctrines, but through presence. The way the evening light kissed the temple spire, the way the wind moved through the banyan leaves, the way silence gathered after Guruji's last words — all became part of the teaching.

May this book serve as a companion on your inward pilgrimage.

Not to instruct, but to remind.

Not to give answers, but to awaken seeing.

For when gratitude returns to the heart, life ceases to be a sequence of events — it becomes a sacred continuum, where every breath, every glance, every silence is a doorway back to grace.

And in that stillness — beneath all striving and seeking — you will find what was never lost: the quiet, luminous truth of belonging.

Warm regards,

Shree Shambav

Prelude

The First Step of Remembering

Every deeper journey begins not with new directions, but with a conscious return — a deliberate pause to recognise the layers of life that often go unnoticed. Before gratitude evolves into mastery, it begins as a gentle whisper within, a quiet realisation that life has been speaking to us not only through moments we celebrated but also through trials we resisted and shadows we avoided.

In this second volume, we move beyond the foundations of gratitude and into its alchemy — its power to transform the unseen, the subtle, and the energetic dimensions of our lives. We begin to see that true gratitude does not only dwell in the bright and joyous days. It also lives in uncertainty, in the resistance of the heart, in the moments that challenge us to grow, to soften, and to awaken. It calls us to honour life in its entirety — light and shadow, triumph and struggle, clarity and confusion.

This book is not a manual, nor a prescription. It is a mirror. A mirror that reflects the deeper art of being awake to life — recognising how gratitude interacts with relationships, with nature, with our inner frequencies, and with the subtle currents of energy that ripple through every choice, every thought, every interaction. Each chapter is an invitation to move from acknowledgement to mastery, guiding you from understanding gratitude intellectually to embodying it as a dynamic, living presence.

In this volume, the focus is on transformation. You will explore how resistance and ingratitude arise, how energetic alignment shapes perception, and how daily, intentional practices can tune your vibration, attuning you more deeply to life's flow. Through stories, reflections, and practical exercises, you will see how gratitude, when consciously applied, amplifies love, resilience, and presence.

As you journey through these pages, you may notice subtle but profound shifts. The mind becomes clearer, the heart more open, and the world around you more vibrant and responsive. Ordinary experiences begin to reveal their hidden depths, and challenges transform into opportunities for awakening. The seemingly small acts — a mindful pause, a heartfelt acknowledgement, a gentle breath — become catalysts for alignment with life itself.

The purpose of this volume is not only to teach gratitude but to guide its conscious embodiment.

When gratitude becomes energetic, relational, and reflective, life itself responds in harmony. Every moment becomes a doorway to understanding, every interaction a reflection of deeper truth, and every breath a bridge to presence and peace.

This is the first step of remembering in the alchemy of gratitude — a deliberate, conscious return to awareness, presence, and resonance. From this awakened state, the deeper art of living unfolds, and life transforms into a continuous flow of grace, wonder, and boundless appreciation.

At Kanchipuram

"The true sunrise is not in the sky but in the silence that breaks within us. Every ray of light that touches the Earth first seeks to awaken the heart."

- Shree Shambav.

The Morning in Kanchipuram

The morning in Kanchipuram carried a subtle hush, as if the town itself had exhaled a long-held breath of anticipation. The rain of the night still clung to every surface: leaves bowed under the weight of dew, temple stones shimmered like wet bronze, and the streets gleamed with the tender reflection of a sky not yet fully awake. The sun lingered behind the soft veil of dawn, not in haste, but in patient ceremony, waiting to arrive as one waits for a sacred guest, draped in reverence and gold.

A cool breeze wandered through the temple streets, carrying the fragrance of wet earth, mingled with the lingering sweetness of jasmine that had survived the night's drizzle. The riverlets, modest in their flow after the rain, hummed quiet, eternal songs, threading water through stone as if narrating secrets of creation. Trees, stoic and timeless, swayed gently, droplets on their leaves trembling like a heartbeat in the cool morning air.

Akshaya, Padma, Vasudeva, and Vidyarthi, emerging from their morning meditation, moved with unhurried grace, the kind that comes from aligning breath with the rhythm of existence. Their steps were soft upon the wet stones, yet carried the weight of presence, each stride a silent acknowledgement that the world, in all its unfolding, was already complete. Slowly, the first rays of the sun touched the horizon, delicate as a painter's brush on silk, while birds perched in poised stillness, as if holding notes that had been waiting since the dawn of time.

By the Brindavan Garden, Aastha, Abhirami, Kiran, Sam, and Alice meandered among flowers that swayed like dancers attuned to an invisible raga. Dewdrops clung to petals as though reluctant to release the night's embrace, glimmering like tiny suspended worlds. From the temple steps, Akshatha, Nita, Lalitha, Rohith, and Sujitha arrived, their voices from bhajan lingering like sacred incense, weaving a soundscape of devotion into the very air. Soon after, Roopa, Kieron, Astyn, Espen, Greta, and Divyani appeared, warmed from their yoga practice, carrying the silent song of breath and alignment in their poised forms. This was not merely the arrival of day—it was a homecoming. The sun did not rise; it arrived, offering radiance not as light alone, but as the gift of being seen, of being remembered.

Sofia, Bhavya, and Akanksh walked along the gravel path—not as mere wanderers, but as pilgrims answering a call older than their names. The breeze through neem leaves became the soft drone of a tanpura, tuning the very air for a raga yet unsung. Even the ancient banyans seemed to bow with centuries of memory, welcoming the returning souls. Their steps bore the imprint of belonging—not granted, but awakened, a silent recognition of life's intimate choreography. Silence walked with them, not absence, but presence—a companion in the sacred geometry of the moment.

Then, as though the universe itself conspired to soften the heart, Aarna smiled. "Shall we begin with coffee?" she asked, her voice a gentle bell of warmth. More than a suggestion, it was an opening, a ritual of shared humanity. In their hands, cups glowed like tiny lamps, radiating warmth through fingers, through breath, through quiet anticipation.

Birdsong rose, slow and devotional, an alaap of the morning raga. The fragrance of sandalwood interwove with the subtle aroma of neem blossoms, and the garden became a living puja, a space where laughter and devotion danced together effortlessly. Aarna, Dev, and John joined, bringing with them sunlight in sound—gentle, effortless, sincere.

Roopa's voice cut softly through the gentle murmur, reverent, "Guruji would be continuing on *Mastering the Art of Gratitude*—a journey from acknowledgement to awakening." Heads nodded in quiet recognition, the smallest ripples of readiness spreading through the circle.

Then came the hush. Not the hush of emptiness, but of fullness—the weightless awareness that life itself was listening. Apeksha lifted her gaze to the banyan canopy, golden light spilling through the leaves like molten silk, the sky soft and inviting. When her eyes returned to the circle, something subtle yet profound had shifted, as though an unseen door, hidden in the folds of time, had quietly opened.

Before words could form, Nita's voice emerged, low and reverent, almost a vibration of the morning air itself. "Apeksha," she said, "please… narrate a story to begin our day."

The Lamp and the Rain

Apeksha closed her eyes for a moment. The garden seemed to lean in — even the breeze paused at the hem of her sari. When she spoke, her voice was not hurried; it carried the rhythm of someone remembering rather than reciting.

"Last night," she began softly, "as the rain fell, I watched a small oil lamp flickering in the shrine outside my room. The wind was strong; the flame trembled, swayed, and almost went out. I thought to shelter it — but something in me whispered, *wait.*

So I watched. Every drop of rain that touched the lamp's edge became a test of endurance. The flame would bend, shrink, then rise again. And in that fragile dance, I saw the story of the heart."

The group listened — still, yet alive.

Apeksha continued, "We often think strength means resistance. But last night, I learned — true strength is tenderness that refuses to disappear. The lamp didn't fight the rain; it yielded, it bent, but it never forgot its purpose — to give light.

Gratitude, I realised, is just like that flame. It does not deny the storm. It survives *because* of it. Every challenge, every loss, every unspoken ache — they are the rain that teaches the lamp how to shine without pride."

Her eyes opened slowly, reflecting the morning sun now fully risen above the temple dome.

"When the rain finally stopped," she said, "I saw that the lamp was smaller, its oil nearly spent — but the flame still danced. And in that gentle light, the wet earth glittered as though the entire world had joined in its devotion.

That's when I understood — gratitude is not the joy that follows fulfilment. It is the quiet light that endures through uncertainty, the remembrance that life, even when trembling, is holy."

For a long while, no one spoke. The banyans rustled lightly, as though in benediction.

Then Padma whispered, "Perhaps that's why Guruji says — *when we bow in gratitude, we do not surrender; we awaken.*"

The silence that followed was not empty — it was full, sacred, like a prayer completed.

After a long, contemplative pause, Abhilasha exhaled—a soft sigh, rich with contentment. "It's time for Guruji's morning session," she said, and the circle, now fully awake, settled into the sacred rhythm of Kanchipuram. The morning, the city, the earth, and all beings within it seemed to breathe together—a single, living invocation to presence, gratitude, and the subtle art of arrival.

Note: Hereafter, Shree Shambav will be referred to as 'Guruji' means Master.

PART ONE

Foundations of Gratitude

The Heart of Belonging

"Every relationship is a reflection of the divine — revealing where we love freely and where we still withhold love. Gratitude turns that mirror into a window through which we see the sacred in others."

\- *Shree Shambav*

CHAPTER I

Gratitude and Relationships

"Nature does not speak in words but in whispers — the rustle of leaves, the rhythm of rain, the stillness of dawn. Gratitude is the ear that hears her hymn."

– Shree Shambav.

Synopsis

Gratitude deepens when it extends beyond the self and touches the hearts of others. This chapter explores how relationships—family, friends, colleagues, and even strangers—become mirrors and teachers, revealing lessons in patience, compassion, and connection. Every interaction, whether joyous or challenging, carries a hidden gift, waiting to be recognised.

By cultivating gratitude in relationships, we transform ordinary moments into extraordinary experiences. A kind word, a shared silence, or even a disagreement can become opportunities for growth and reflection. Recognising the divine spark in others shifts perception from judgment to appreciation, from expectation to acceptance.

Readers are guided through practical exercises such as reflective journaling, expressing thanks aloud, and mindful listening. The chapter emphasises empathy, understanding, and acknowledgement of the unseen efforts and love that surround us daily.

Ultimately, gratitude in relationships nurtures both self-awareness and connection, creating bonds grounded in respect and reverence. By thanking others—not just for what they do but for who they are—we align with the universal truth: love is both given and received. Through this practice, life becomes a network of sacred encounters, each infused with meaning, joy, and the quiet beauty of shared existence.

The Gift of Presence

Guruji's voice settled into the room like a bell whose sound lives on after the strike. "Seeing beyond the mask," he began, "is the simplest and most radical act of love. It asks nothing of the other but to be seen — not performed for, not fixed, simply witnessed."

There is a difference between presence and performance. Performance dresses itself in light; it wants applause. Presence sits quietly by the window with no need to be noticed — it breathes with the other's breath and learns the shape of their silence.

The Theatre and the Lantern

Imagine a small village theatre. Actors take the stage with elaborate costumes and practised smiles. The audience applauds the gestures; the play is admired. Now imagine, backstage, a single lantern. It is not noticed in reviews or flattered by clapping. Yet its glow allows the actors to find the prop they dropped, to see their lines scribbled on the script, to wipe the sweat from a brow. The lantern's usefulness is hushed, humble, essential.

So too are the unnoticed acts of love — the making of tea at dawn, a quiet hand on a trembling shoulder, the remembering of a name. They do not demand limelight. They sustain the play of life. When we prize performance — the projected face, the polished answer — relationships become reviews. When we honour the lantern, relationships become shelter.

Two Women, A Wall, and a Window

There were two friends, Rita and Latha. Rita was eloquent, impeccable in public; people praised her for always knowing what to say. Latha was quieter, her kindness marked by small practical things: she would leave a book open where Rita last read, mend a torn hem without fuss, show up with rice when winter made the city brittle. One evening, Rita, exhausted after a ceremony where she had spoken well, broke down alone in her courtyard. Mask dropped, she sobbed until there were no words left. Latha came without announcement, placed a warm cloth on Rita's forehead, and sat in silence until dawn.

Rita later said, "I had never believed someone could know me without being told how to act around me." Latha replied, "I never needed you to be anything but yourself for me to be here." What healed Rita was not the praise for her speeches, but the presence that existed before the speech — the knowing without demand. That presence carried Rita back to herself.

Gratitude as a Slow Flame

Gratitude is less like a celebratory firework and more like a slow-burning lamp. Fireworks dazzle and then are gone; the lamp, tended with small acts — trimming the wick, ensuring there is oil — lasts through the night. Presence is the tending. Noticing someone's ordinary efforts — the way they steady a cup with both hands, the way they remember a tiny preference — is the oil poured into the lamp of relationship. Over time, these small observations become warmth, and warmth becomes trust.

Four Ways Presence Transforms Relationship

Recognition over Reaction.

When we recognise (see the person's being) rather than react (respond to the mask), we interrupt the reflex to judge or fix. Presence frees the other from performing to please us.

Witnessing without Editing.

To witness is to hold another's reality without inserting our corrections. It is different from approval; it is receptivity. A witnessed grief feels less monstrous; a witnessed joy expands.

The Practice of Small Notices.

Gratitude grows when we catalogue tiny mercies: the way someone laughs, their habitual pause before answering, the tiredness at the corner of their smile. These notices are a map of the person's inner landscape.

Holding Space, Not Solving Space.

Presence often looks like doing nothing. It means offering a container where someone can unfold. Solving is seductive; holding is brave.

How to Begin Practising Presence Today

One Small Inventory: Each evening, name three small things someone did for you that day. Don't judge their magnitude — simply name them. Writing these is a balm for the mind trained in performance.

Two-Minute Witness: When someone speaks, practice two uninterrupted minutes of listening. No advice, no story of your own, no rescue. Let silence sit with the words.

The Lantern Gesture: Once a week, do one unseen thing for someone: refill their tea, sweep a corner they use, leave a note of thanks. Do it without mention.

Mirror Check: Before you interact, ask: "Am I seeking to be seen, or to see?" If you find yourself craving recognition, breathe, ground, and choose presence.

Why Presence Is Sacred

When we insist on performance, we teach others to prepare for judgment. When we choose presence, we offer a revolutionary freedom: the permission to be imperfect, to be becoming. In that permission, healing begins. In that freedom, gratitude arises not as a duty but as a natural buoyancy.

The Old Banyan

Guruji said, "At the edge of the ashram stands an old banyan. People come, some to climb its roots, others to shelter beneath its expanse. Over the years, it has known laughter, weeping, and quiet study. No one credits the banyan when meetings succeed; no one blames it when storms fall. Yet without its shade, many small gatherings would have failed. The banyan asks nothing; it simply is. Presence, like the banyan, asks nothing and gives everything. It does not perform; it sustains."

Guruji smiled, and the room softened. "Practice," he said gently, "being the lantern and sitting under the banyan. Let gratitude find you in the small, ordinary moments. Let your presence be the sanctuary where masks can come off and hearts remember how to breathe."

Seeing Beyond the Mask

Alice asked, "Guruji, when was the last time we genuinely acknowledged someone's effort—without expectation, without judgment?"

Guruji turned his gaze toward Alice, his eyes calm, luminous — as if they carried the reflection of still water under morning light. The question lingered in the air like incense smoke, spiralling, delicate, unanswered yet profoundly understood.

He smiled gently. Guruji said, "is one of the most sacred questions you can ask — not of me, but of yourself."

A hush fell upon the gathering.

The Story of the Potter and the Child

Guruji began softly, his voice weaving a story into silence.

"There was once a humble potter who lived by the banks of a river. Every day, before the sun rose, he would knead clay with his weathered hands — strong, cracked, and tired — and whisper prayers into it. His pots were not perfect; some were uneven, some bore the marks of his fingers, but each carried warmth — the kind that only love can shape.

Across his small lane lived a young boy who would watch him every morning. The boy's father, a wealthy merchant, would often mock the potter, saying, 'He's just a poor man playing with mud. What good comes from such labour?'

One day, the boy approached the potter and asked, 'Why do you smile when no one praises you for your work?'

The potter looked up, hands deep in clay, and said, 'Because I see life taking form. That is enough. The river gives me the clay, the sun gives me warmth, and the earth allows me to create. Must the world also applaud for me to be grateful?'

Years passed. The boy grew into a man, carrying that single answer in his heart like an ember that refused to die. Whenever life demanded applause, he would remember the potter's quiet smile — and find peace in his effort rather than in its recognition."

Guruji paused. His eyes swept across the circle — Apeksha, Akshaya, Nita, Alice — each listening not only with ears but with hearts that had begun to tremble awake.

The Unseen Currency of Love

"We live," Guruji said, "in a world that measures value by attention — where gratitude is often delayed until applause is received. But genuine acknowledgement is an invisible act — a silent 'I see you' without expecting 'see me too.'

When we compliment a flower for its fragrance, do we expect it to thank us? When a mother wakes before dawn, boiling milk for her family, she is rarely praised. Yet the warmth in that act sustains life itself.

Gratitude begins in that seeing — in honouring the quiet hands that hold our days together. The cook who adds extra salt because she remembers your taste. The friend who waits a few seconds longer before ending the call. The teacher who silently rephrases the question so you can find your voice. These are the invisible stitches that hold love in place."

Guruji leaned forward slightly, his tone now softer, more intimate.

"Most people are starving, not for food or comfort, but for acknowledgement. We see their performance — their achievements, their failures — but rarely their essence, the small, trembling effort behind it. When we acknowledge effort without judgment, we give someone the most priceless gift: *dignity of being seen.*"

The Mirror in the Temple

Guruji pointed toward the temple dome in the distance. "Do you see that temple mirror?"

Everyone turned. Near the sanctum door was an old brass mirror, its surface worn, its shine softened by time.

"That mirror," Guruji said, "never reflects itself. Yet it receives every face, every flame, every offering. It does not judge who stands before it — rich or poor, joyful or broken — it only reflects what is.

When you acknowledge another's effort purely, you become that mirror. You reflect their light back to them, reminding them of their own worth. And in that moment, something extraordinary happens — gratitude becomes mutual, even if no words are exchanged."

Guruji's gaze returned to Alice. "You asked, *When was the last time we genuinely acknowledged someone's effort?* Perhaps the question is not when, but *how often we failed to.*

There was once a woman who watered a small sapling outside her home every morning. Her neighbours mocked her, saying, 'Why care for such a frail plant?' One day, she fell ill and could not leave her bed. Days passed; the plant dried, its leaves withered. But when the monsoon arrived, something miraculous happened — from its brittle stem, new shoots emerged, green and alive.

Her husband stood by the window and wept. He realised he had never once thanked her — not for the food she cooked, not for the care she gave, not for the love that had always been quietly present. He had been waiting for grand moments, forgetting that love announces itself only in whispers.

Presence over performance, Alice — that is where love lives."

Guruji's tone softened into a whisper — almost a prayer.

"When we acknowledge without expectation, we open a portal to the sacred. It is through that act that souls recognise one another. The performer becomes the presence; the seen becomes the seer.

So before you sleep tonight," he said, "ask your heart — who gave their unseen light to my day today? And can I thank them — not with words, but with awareness?"

The garden was utterly still. The banyan leaves no longer rustled; even the air had bowed in reverence.

Alice's eyes glistened, not with sorrow, but with awakening — the kind that comes when understanding turns into remembrance.

Guruji smiled again, serene. "When acknowledgement becomes your nature," he said, "gratitude ceases to be a practice — it becomes your presence."

Lessons in Love

"Every interaction is a teacher," he said, "and every teacher asks only one thing — pay attention." He folded his hands as if gathering the invisible lessons that drifted between them, then began.

Seeing Difficulty as Curriculum

"We treat joy like prize day and difficulty like detention," Guruji said, "but what if the opposite were true? What if every friction were a classroom, and every wound a text to be read?"

Relationships are not tests to pass or fail, he explained, but mirrors. They return to us not only what we offer, but what we refuse to see. A sting of jealousy, a flare of anger, an ache of abandonment — these are not enemies to exile; they are tutors knocking politely, asking, *What do you still need to learn?*

When we reframe conflict as a curriculum, gratitude follows naturally. We stop counting only what we received and begin to inventory what the encounter taught us — patience, boundary, courage, humility. Gratitude then becomes an orientation: not toward outcomes, but toward learning.

The River That Teaches the Bank

Imagine a river and its bank. When the water flows gently, the bank is content; when the current rages, the bank is reshaped. If the bank resists the flood, it only hardens and breaks. But if the bank studies the river

— the force, the debris, the season — it learns to build terraces, to plant roots that hold. The river's force is not punishment; it is information. So too with difficult people or moments: they are the current that can teach us how to hold our ground more kindly.

Two Houses, One Storm

Guruji said, "There were two neighbouring houses on the same street. One family sealed windows at the first sign of wind, bolted doors, and cursed the weather. The other family lit lamps, opened cupboards to shelter neighbours, and harvested rainwater. After the storm, the first found their shutters broken and their trust eroded; the second found newly formed friendships and a pantry refilled by shared care."

The difference was not in the storm — it was in the interpretation. The first treated difficulty as an enemy to be feared; the second treated it as a teacher whose assignments included compassion and resourcefulness.

The Conversation as Lesson (Pairs / Circle)

This exercise turns a real or recent difficult interaction into a classroom. Use it in pairs or as a small group.

- **Recall (3 mins, silent).** Each person holds one difficult recent interaction in mind. Keep names and blame aside; focus on the interaction's feeling.
- **Tell the Story (5 mins each).** One person speaks for five uninterrupted minutes about what happened — no defence, no justification, just the experience. The other listens as a student: curious, non-reactive.
- **Teach-Back (3 mins).** The listener summarises what they heard and names one possible lesson the interaction contains for the speaker (not advice; a perceived learning).
- **Reflection (2 mins).** The speaker receives the teach-back, then says whether it resonates and what they might do differently next time.
- **Gratitude Close (1 min).** End by naming one thing you're grateful for about the other — not for what they did, but for who they are in this learning.

This practice trains witnessing over reacting and converts grievance energy into inquiry.

Micro-Practices — Daily Habits that Turn Interaction into Insight

- **The Two-Question Pause:** After any charged exchange, wait two heartbeats and ask yourself privately: 1) What did this reveal about me? 2) What does it ask me to become? Write one-word answers.

- **The Mirror Note:** Each week, write a short note to someone who pushed your buttons and thank them for one thing they unknowingly taught you. Send it only if it feels safe; otherwise, keep it as a private offering.

- **Gratitude for the Mirror:** Each evening, list one tough moment and write the single skill it taught you (patience, clarity, boundary-setting). Small lists build big humility.

A Seeker's Lesson

Guruji said, "Let me narrate a story. Sahana approached a monk after a heated conversation with her brother. Her voice still quivered. "He accused me of being cold," she said. "I want to prove him wrong."

Monk looked at her kindly. "Prove nothing," he said. "Learn everything."

Sahana frowned. "How is that even fair?"

"Fairness is a child of understanding," Monk replied. "Ask: what in you tightened when he spoke? Was it a wound he hit, or a habit of armour you have been wearing so long you forgot it is there?"

Sahana sat with the question. The next morning, she called her brother not to defend, but to ask what had hurt him. In his answering — awkward, tearful, honest — she discovered not attack but loneliness. The conversation changed. The shift wasn't dramatic; it was steady.

Group Exercise — "The Mirror Circle"

- Form a circle. Each person names a recent mirror (a person or event that reflected something difficult).
- One by one, the group offers one sentence of observation (no solutions) about what virtue the mirror might be asking the person to develop. Keep tone tender.
- The named person receives, then names one tiny practice they'll try for a week.
- Close with three breaths together, acknowledging that learning is never hurried.

Every difficult encounter is an invitation to enlarge the heart's capacity. When we practice learning instead of defending, gratitude grows not because life is easy, but because we become stronger learners of love.

Guruji said, "Sit quietly for five breaths. Picture someone who recently upset you. Breathe in the image. On the out-breath, silently say, "Teacher." Repeat for five breaths. Notice what softens. This tiny word maps a new relationship to difficulty: from enemy to instructor."

Guruji folded his hands, and the garden held its breath. "If every human is a teacher," he said softly, "then the question is not who hurts me, but what lesson do I refuse to learn?" He smiled, not to soothe, but to invite courage. "Learn bravely. Love unworried by outcome. And let gratitude be the bell you ring at every class."

Every Interaction is a Teacher

Guruji smiled — a knowing, quiet smile that often appeared before he shared something that seemed to touch the soul directly. The morning light streamed through the tall windows of the hall, scattering gold across the marble floor. A soft silence settled before he replied, as if even the air wanted to listen.

Sofia's question lingered — *Can we remember a challenging encounter that ultimately taught us patience, compassion, or understanding?*

Guruji leaned slightly forward, his voice gentle yet steady, "Yes, Sofia… such moments are the true classrooms of the heart."

He paused and then said, "Let me tell you a story — about a monk named Raghav, who once believed he was deeply patient and compassionate. Until one day, life decided to test the truth of his belief."

Raghav and the Farmer

Raghav lived in a small hermitage on the outskirts of a village. Every morning, he would meditate by the river, and every evening, he would teach those who came seeking peace. He was calm, soft-spoken, and disciplined. Villagers respected him deeply.

But one day, a farmer came to his hut — frustrated, angry, and restless. He complained about his failing crops, his disobedient sons, and how his wife no longer cared for him. Raghav listened patiently and offered words of comfort. Yet, the farmer kept returning, day after day, with louder complaints and sharper words.

At first, Raghav endured. But soon, his calm began to crack.
He found himself irritated, even resentful.

"Why does he come here only to pour his misery?" he thought.
"Why can't he find peace himself?"

One evening, when the farmer began yet another long tirade, Raghav's patience broke. He stood and said sharply, “Enough! I am not here to solve your endless problems. Go find your answers elsewhere.”

The farmer’s face fell. He nodded silently and left.

That night, Raghav could not meditate. The stillness of his mind was replaced by guilt. The echo of his own voice — filled with judgment — haunted him.

When he finally closed his eyes, he saw an image — the same farmer, but this time, bent over his dry field, working tirelessly to bring life to the barren soil. A voice within whispered, *You see only his noise, not his pain.*

The next morning, Raghav went to the farmer’s field. The man was there, trying to lift a broken plough. Without a word, Raghav helped him. They worked together under the rising sun, and in that silent labour, something shifted.

When they finished, the farmer looked up, his eyes moist.
“Forgive me, Master,” he said. “I came to you not because I wanted peace, but because I had forgotten what peace feels like.”

Raghav bowed, his heart humbled. “No,” he replied softly, “Forgive *me.* I came to teach, but you came to remind me what compassion truly means.”

Guruji looked around the hall. Everyone was quiet — listening not just to his words, but to the silence between them.

He continued, "You see, Sofia, life often disguises our greatest teachers as the ones who irritate us, oppose us, or exhaust us. The people who test our patience are not obstacles — they are mirrors showing where our love still hesitates."

Then he added, with warmth and clarity, "Every difficult encounter whispers a truth: *You have more compassion to give. You have more peace to discover.* Gratitude helps us see that. Instead of asking, 'Why is this happening to me?' we begin to ask, 'What is this teaching me?'"

Sofia lowered her gaze, smiling faintly, her eyes glistening. The others sat in reflective silence — some remembering their own "farmers," those who had unknowingly refined their hearts.

Guruji concluded softly, "When we bow in gratitude even for those who challenge us, love ceases to be selective — it becomes wise. And that is when relationships stop being transactions… and turn into transformations."

Every Interaction is a Teacher

Expressing Thanks

The morning in Shambav Hall felt weightless — like the world itself had paused to listen. The scent of sandalwood lingered in the air. The devotees sat in stillness, their hearts open after the earlier stories. Then Guruji's voice — calm, unhurried, carrying both gentleness and gravity — rose once more.

"Let us speak," he said softly, "about **Expressing Thanks — The Power of Acknowledgment.**"

He looked around the circle — at Apeksha, Sofia, Nita, and the others — each one holding stories within, each carrying unspoken gratitude that rarely found words.

The Power of Acknowledgement

"Gratitude," Guruji began, "is like a lamp. But acknowledgement… is the act of lighting it."

He paused, letting the sentence rest in the quiet.

"Unexpressed gratitude," he continued, "is like keeping the flame hidden beneath a bowl. The light is there, but no one can see it — not even you. Only when we express our thankfulness — through a word, a letter, a look, or even silence offered with love — does that inner flame begin to illuminate hearts around us."

He then told a story.

The Story of the Potter's Apprentice

"In a small village near Varanasi," Guruji said, "there lived an old potter named Hari Das and his young apprentice, Dev.

Hari Das was patient, meticulous — every pot he shaped seemed to carry a soul of its own. Dev, on the other hand, was eager, often rushing through his work, never quite satisfied.

One day, a travelling merchant came to buy the pots. He looked at the old potter's creations with admiration, then glanced at Dev's and nodded indifferently. Dev's heart sank.

That evening, as they closed the workshop, Hari Das noticed Dev's silence.

'What troubles you, child?' he asked.

Dev replied bitterly, 'I work every day, yet no one praises me. You receive all the gratitude. What am I doing wrong?'

The old potter smiled faintly, walked to the corner, and handed Dev a small pot — one of Dev's earliest creations. It was uneven, slightly cracked, but still whole.

'I have kept this,' Hari Das said, 'because it reminds me of your journey — of the day you first shaped earth into form. You did not see the beauty in your struggle, but I did.'

Tears welled up in Dev's eyes. He had never been thanked — not even by his own father. And yet, here was his master acknowledging not perfection, but *effort.*

The next morning, Dev came early. His touch on the clay was slower, humbler, filled with presence.

In time, his pots began to breathe grace.

Years later, when Hari Das passed away, villagers found hundreds of small pots in his hut — each imperfect, each with a student's name etched below. He had thanked every one of them silently, shaping their confidence even when their hands were still learning."

Guruji looked around the hall. The story had softened every face.

He continued in a tender tone, "Many relationships fade not because love disappears, but because acknowledgement does. A word of appreciation can water the roots of connection. When we say, 'I see your effort,' 'I feel your kindness,' or simply, 'Thank you for being,' we restore dignity to the invisible acts that sustain our lives."

He drew an analogy:

"A river does not hoard its water. It flows, and that flow sustains life. Gratitude, too, must flow. If we keep it locked within, it stagnates. But when we express it — it nourishes hearts, deepens trust, and turns ordinary relationships into sacred companionships."

Apeksha whispered softly, "Guruji, sometimes we feel gratitude, but words seem small. How do we express what we truly feel?"

Guruji smiled. "When words fall short, let your actions speak. A hand on a shoulder, a sincere gaze, a small note left without expectation — these are languages of the heart. Gratitude is not measured by eloquence, but by sincerity. What matters is not how much you say, but how deeply you mean it."

He paused again — the hall utterly still.

Then he concluded, his voice low and luminous: "When you acknowledge another, you remind them — and yourself — that love is alive. Each 'thank you' is a thread in the vast tapestry of human connection. And every time we express it, we become co-creators in the quiet art of healing the world."

Weaving Gratitude into Daily Life

Bhavya asked, "Guruji, how might we weave daily acts of gratitude into our lives, honouring even the smallest gestures of those around us?"

Guruji's eyes softened when Bhavya asked, as if the question itself were a small offering. "To weave gratitude into life," he said, "is to stitch the heart's fabric one careful knot at a time. It is not a grand festival but a quiet, persistent tending." He folded his hands and began, voice low like a bell you can hear long after it rings.

The Woman with the Little Basket

There was once a woman who carried a small woven basket everywhere. She wasn't rich, but every morning she set aside three tiny things for others: a mango for the widow next door, a ribbon for the schoolgirl who swept the temple steps, a handful of rice for the temple sparrows. People noticed her basket and called her generous, but she would only smile and say, "I keep my heart light this way."

Years later, when drought came and food grew scarce, the village remembered the woman's small offerings. The widow came daily to sit by her door and share stories; the schoolgirl, grown into a teacher, taught the children to mend rather than waste; the sparrows returned like a small blessing each morning. The little basket had become a memory-archive of care; those small, repeated habits had created a reservoir of reciprocity and tenderness.

Guruji looked at Bhavya and said, "This is how gratitude lives — in a basket of small things repeated until they become the bedrock of a life."

How Gratitude Actually Grows

- **Start Small.** Big gestures are beautiful; tiny ones are sustainable.
- **Notice First.** You cannot thank what you do not see. Train the eye to find the ordinary.
- **Express Often.** Saying "thank you" is fertiliser: it helps the root take hold.
- **Make it Visible.** Rituals, notes, jars, and lists create a structure that memory alone cannot hold.
- **Be Specific.** "Thank you" gains power when paired with what was noticed: "Thank you for remembering my tea the way I like it."

Practical Daily Practices (Simple, Repeatable)

Three Tiny Thanks (Morning): Each morning, name aloud — or in a journal — three small things someone did for you yesterday. No hierarchy; a smile equals saving a life for this practice.

The Lantern Habit (Midday): Once before lunch, send one short message of appreciation (text, voice note, or sticky note) to someone: a colleague, a vendor, the maid, a friend. Keep it under two sentences.

Evening Witness (Before Sleep): In a single sentence, record one moment you overlooked during the day and what it meant. Example: "Ramesh refilled my water without me asking — he sees when I'm tired."

Weekly Gratitude Gesture: Once a week, perform an unannounced small act for someone — refill a supply, wash a cup, leave a sweet — and let it be anonymous if that feels truer.

Rituals & Physical Tools (Make Gratitude Tangible)

The Gratitude Jar: Each day drop a folded note naming one person and why you're grateful. At month's end, read them aloud with a friend or alone as a blessing.

The Thank-You Template: Keep a one-line template in your phone: "Thank you, ___, for ___. It meant ___." Fill it and send. Specificity reduces hesitation.

The Two-Minute Note: Keep index cards and a pen. Twice a week, write a short handwritten note (no more than 30 words) and leave it where the person will find it. Handwriting carries extra warmth.

A Gratitude Corner: A small shelf with a candle, a stone, and a notebook. Light the candle when you remember someone, and write one line before blowing it out.

Practices for Close Relationships (Deepening, Not Performance)

The Presence Check: Once a day, look at your partner or friend and silently name one thing they did today you appreciate. Hold that image for ten breaths. No need to speak it if the holding changes you.

Repair Script: When tension arises, the first sentence you offer is a gratitude line: "I'm grateful you told me what you felt — I want to hear more." This lowers defences and invites learning.

Re-storying: When you recall a difficult person, deliberately remind yourself of one small kindness they offered earlier. This balances the mirror and prevents gratitude from becoming conditional.

Community & Work (Small Culture Shifts)

Start Meetings With Thanks: Begin team meetings by naming one success and one person who made it possible. Three minutes of gratitude shifts tone and increases trust.

Shared Thank-You Board: In a home or office, put up a board for quick "thank you" notes. Reading them later sustains morale.

Monthly Gratitude Circle: A short monthly gathering (15–20 mins) where people speak a single thanks aloud. Ritualises appreciation and bonds the group.

How to Speak Thanks So it Heals

Use **specifics**: "Thank you for bringing the extra blanket; I slept better."

Express **impact**: "When you did that, I felt lighter and seen."

Offer **no strings**: Avoid "I'll return the favour" as the primary close; let gratitude be its own abundance.

Include **acknowledgment of effort**: "I know it took time—thank you for staying late."

Dealing with Resistance — When Gratitude Feels Forced

Start privately: If saying thanks aloud feels performative, journal it first. Let authenticity grow.

Notice expectation. If you find yourself thanking to get something back, pause and reframe: "I'll offer this without a ledger."

Accept imperfect returns: Sometimes gratitude is a seed that flowers later, not instantly. Remember the woman with the basket.

A Short Guided Practice (Five Minutes)

Sit comfortably. Close your eyes. Breathe three slow breaths.

Bring to mind someone who did something small today. See the action clearly.

Feel where in your body gratitude lives — a warmth, a lift, a softening. Breathe into it.

Silently say their name and one word of thanks. Hold for three breaths.

Open your eyes; if possible, send them a one-line message: “I noticed and I’m grateful.”

How Small Acts Compound

Guruji said, “Years after the woman with the little basket had died, the village met to repair the temple roof. No one had a plan until the teacher of the school remembered the woman’s habit. He suggested they each bring one small thing to help: a plank, a tin of nails, a cooked meal. The day became a festival of humble giving. People discovered that small gifts accumulated into shelter, and in that building they experienced gratitude as architecture. What began as tiny daily acts had grown into the village’s capacity to care for itself.”

Guruji said, “Notice how simple repetitions built a refuge. Gratitude is not merely a feeling; it is an infrastructure we build together.”

A Month of Micro-Tasks

If Bhavya wishes to begin today, Guruji offered a gentle map for thirty days:

Week 1: Practice **Three Tiny Thanks** each morning.

Week 2: Add the **Lantern Habit** midday messages.

Week 3: Begin the **Gratitude Jar** at home.

Week 4: Host or join a **Gratitude Circle** and share one story.
At month's end, sit with your jar. Read the notes. Notice how the world looks different.

"Remember," he said softly, "we do not invent gratitude; we remember it. The world is already full of reasons to be thankful. Our task is simply to keep our hands busy: weave a stitch each day, and soon enough you will see the whole cloth."

The Divine in Others

Guruji's voice softened the room as if a veil had been drawn back. "To see the divine in another," he said, "is not a mystical privilege reserved for saints. It is a radical way of looking — a small, steady discipline that transforms how we meet the world."

He paused, letting the sentence settle like light on water.

The River and the Pearl

Guruji after a pause said, "Imagine a river that carries both mud and pearls. If you judge the river by its silt, you will curse its murk. If you look carefully, you may find pearls hidden within. People, like rivers, carry both clumsy acts and buried light. To see the pearl is not to ignore the silt; it is to hold both with humility — to understand that the same current that stirred the mud also polished the pearl into being."

The Washerman and the Crown

Once, in a small town, a young prince lost his ceremonial crown in the river. The whole court panicked; the crown represented lineage, dignity, and the weight of rule. Many searched the palace and blamed the palace-keepers, but none found it.

A humble washerman, who cleaned clothes by the river, returned to the shore at dusk and noticed a glint beneath the surface. He waded in, hands cold and steady, and brought up the crown, wrapped it in a scrap of cloth, and carried it back to the palace. No fanfare followed; he slipped away to his home with the satisfaction of a task done.

When the king learned who had found the crown, he wanted to honour the washerman with gold and ceremony. The washerman refused; he only asked that his children be allowed to study and that his neighbour's family receive a month's grain.

The king was puzzled. "Why refuse personal reward?" he asked.

The washerman looked down at his rough hands and said, "The river gives me work. I do not need gold to know I am enough. I only ask that others have what they need."

In that refusal, the king saw a quiet enormity — a testament that dignity and service are different forms of the same light. The washerman's act revealed a soul not in need of recognition to be whole. The king, humbled, learned to see beyond rank and ceremony to the sacredness in ordinary labour.

How Gratitude Reveals Sacredness

It Shifts the Question: From "What did they do?" to "Who are they beneath what they did?"

It Lowers the Guard: Gratitude invites curiosity instead of defence; curiosity invites story instead of verdict.

It Restores Dignity: Naming effort and being — "I see you" — returns worth to the person who may have been reduced to a role.

It Deepens Relationship: When people feel seen at essence, trust grows and masks relax.

Small Ways to Train the Eye

The Three-Depth Pause (Before Reaction): When you're about to judge, pause for three breaths. Ask: 1) What happened? 2) What might be the hidden need or story here? 3) One grateful observation about this person. Respond from that softer place.

The Hidden-Story Question: Instead of "Why did you do that?" try, "Help me see what led you there." It invites context without accusation.

The Daily Sacred-List: Each evening, list one thing you saw in someone today that felt generous, brave, or true even if it was small or unseen. Keep this list for a month and revisit it.

The Ritual of Return: If you have been quick to judge someone, return with a small acknowledgement: a note, a word, or a silent bow. "I saw you differently today" can heal surprising distance.

The Garden and the Weeds

Guruji said, "A gardener who only praises blooms misses the intelligence of the soil. Weeds signal imbalance, compacted earth, or hidden pests. A wise gardener thanks both blooms and weeds — tending to what is broken and celebrating what is flourishing. Similarly, seeing the divine in others means neither sentimentalising pain nor ignoring harm; it means caring for the whole garden, recognising the seed even in the thorn.

Vasudeva asked, "But Guruji, what about those who harm others? How do we see divinity there?" Guruji smiled and said, "Seeing the divine is not excusing harm. It is knowing there is more than the harm, even within the harmed-maker. Compassion with boundaries: protect the vulnerable, speak truth, but do not collapse your heart into hatred. Sometimes the most difficult people are the loudest teachers of what we must not become."

How to Practice in Difficult Situations

Safeguard First: If someone is dangerous or abusive, ensure safety and set boundaries. Seeing the divine does not replace protection.

Contain the Story: Name the action factually. Then, in private, imagine the hidden story — illness, fear, pressure — to cultivate empathy.

Act Justly, Love Fiercely: Justice and compassion can coexist. Take firm action when needed; allow space for rehabilitation where possible.

Closure with Clarity: If reconciliation isn't possible, offer a brief inner blessing: "May you find the light you still seek," and continue your care for yourself.

Five Breaths to See Deeper

Sit quietly. Bring to mind someone whose action recently annoyed you.

Breathe in, naming the action. Breathe out, releasing immediate judgment.

Breathe in, imagine one hidden fact about their life (a burden, a fear, a small kindness). Breathe out, soften.

Repeat three times. Conclude with one sentence of gratitude for them — even if it is simply: "Thank you for being a mirror for my patience."

The Lamp Maker's Gift

An old lamp maker carved simple clay lamps. One evening he gave his last lamp to a child who had nothing to light. The child lit the lamp, and for the first time, the lamp maker saw the child's face glow with a dignity the world had denied him. The lamp maker's hands were cracked and ink-stained, but his chest warmed. He turned to his apprentice and said quietly,

"We make light not to be seen, but so others can see themselves."

Seeing the divine in others is like making lamps for one another. Every acknowledgement, every act of gratitude, is an offering that helps another see themselves as more than their mistakes, more than their roles — as someone touched by a universal light.

Aarna asked, "Guruji, who in our lives might we begin to see with fresh eyes, recognizing the light within them rather than dwelling on their faults?"

Guruji smiled gently, his gaze steady yet filled with the softness of someone who has seen through countless hearts. The hall was still; even the flickering flame of the lamp seemed to listen.

He said, "Aarna, your question touches the essence of divine seeing — the ability to look beyond form, beyond behaviour, beyond the layers of misunderstanding that cloud the truth of who someone is. Every soul carries the same light — some shine clearly, some are veiled by pain, and some are hidden beneath the dust of ego and hurt. But the light remains — unaltered, unbroken, pure."

He paused, and his eyes drifted to the window where the evening sun melted into a golden horizon. "You see, life often tests us through the mirrors it holds up

— people we find difficult, stubborn, or indifferent. They are not obstacles; they are teachers cloaked in disguise. Their presence stirs something within us that calls for healing — impatience, judgment, resentment, pride. When we learn to see *them* not as 'the difficult ones,' but as reflections awakening our dormant compassion, gratitude blossoms naturally."

He turned toward Aarna. "Think of your father, your friend, or perhaps someone who misunderstood you. What if, instead of reacting to their behaviour, you paused and whispered inwardly — *'Here too, the Divine resides.'* This simple remembrance transforms perception. You begin to *see* rather than merely look. Gratitude is born not from what they do, but from what they awaken in you."

The devotees were silent, moved. The air was charged with the weight of realisation.

Guruji said, his voice low and tender, "In a forest, each tree grows differently. Some stand tall and proud, some are twisted and scarred, yet each one reaches for the same sun. Likewise, each person you meet is on their own path of reaching — struggling, learning, remembering. When you see their journey instead of their flaws, compassion replaces criticism, and gratitude flows like a gentle stream."

He smiled faintly, "Start with one person who feels hard to love. Look into their eyes, even if only in your heart, and say — '*I honour the light in you, even if you cannot yet see it yourself.*' That acknowledgment alone begins to heal unseen wounds — in them and in you. Seeing the Divine in others is not about excusing their actions; it is about remembering their essence."

Aarna's eyes glistened. She whispered, "Guruji... perhaps that is what true love is — seeing with the eyes of the soul."

Guruji nodded, "Yes, my child. To see the Divine in others is to see God learning to love Himself through a thousand forms — and gratitude is the prayer that keeps that vision alive."

The silence in the hall deepened as Guruji's voice slowed, his tone tender, as though the story itself carried an invisible blessing. The devotees leaned forward, drawn into the luminous space where his words wove spirit into life.

Guruji said softly, "Let me narrate a story — *The Weaver and the Stranger.*

In a small, bustling village lived a weaver named Elara. Her fingers danced tirelessly over threads of every colour, creating tapestries that told stories of seasons, prayers, and dreams. She was known for her precision — every thread in its place, every colour in balance. Yet, beneath her calm rhythm was a quiet ache — a sense that something in life was beautifully crafted but incomplete."

He paused, letting the stillness stretch like a sacred pause in music.

"One day," Guruji went on, "Elara began to notice a stranger. Each morning, as she set up her stall in the village market, he would appear — standing silently at a distance, watching. He never bought anything, never spoke, never gestured. The villagers laughed, whispering that he was peculiar or perhaps lost. But Elara… she saw something different. His eyes carried both distance and depth, as if he were seeing a world beyond the one around them."

"One afternoon, as rain poured unexpectedly, Elara saw the stranger standing unprotected beneath the storm. Without a thought, she called out, 'Come, shelter here!' He hesitated, but eventually stepped under her awning, dripping wet and silent. Moments passed before he reached into his satchel and handed her a small woven charm — simple, made of coarse fibre and dyed in faded hues. He spoke only one sentence — *'For your kindness, may your threads never break.'* Then he left."

Guruji's eyes softened as he looked around the hall. "Elara did not understand. The charm looked ordinary, almost worn. Yet something about it felt alive, humming faintly with warmth. She hung it above her loom — not for beauty, but as remembrance of that moment of silent connection."

He leaned forward, his voice growing more intimate. "Weeks passed. Business slowed, debts mounted, and worry clouded her heart. Then, without warning, a large order arrived from a distant merchant — enough to sustain her workshop for months. As she sat that evening under the charm's gentle sway, Elara smiled. It was not about magic or coincidence — it was the unseen thread of grace moving through human hearts."

Guruji's tone deepened, now carrying a tender weight of truth. "Elara realised that gratitude is not for what we *gain* but for what we *recognise.* The stranger's presence had reminded her that every soul we meet carries unseen blessings — sometimes in silence, sometimes through trials, sometimes through simple gestures. Gratitude allows us to see those invisible weavers who hold our lives together."

He looked around the hall, eyes resting on each devotee as if his gaze touched their hearts one by one. "Each relationship, is a thread in the grand tapestry of existence. Some threads are bright — bringing joy, laughter, and ease. Others are dark — bringing pain, challenge, and depth. But both are needed for the pattern to be whole. Gratitude is the art of seeing how every thread — visible or hidden — contributes to the design of our destiny."

He smiled gently. "When we honour even the smallest presence, we begin to see the divine weaver behind every encounter — the stranger, the friend, the rival, the beloved. They are all parts of the same cosmic loom."

The devotees sat in silence. The lamp's flame flickered, casting soft golden shadows that seemed to ripple across the floor like woven light. Guruji's final words lingered in the air:

"Remember, my dear ones — life is the tapestry, love is the thread, and gratitude… gratitude is the eye that sees the beauty of the weave."

The midday sun hovered gently above the horizon, soft yet bright, spilling a golden warmth over the grounds of Shambav Hall. After a long pause, Guruji's voice broke the stillness, calm yet carrying quiet authority.

"Let us take our midday meal," he said.

The devotees rose slowly, almost in unison, as if each step was part of a shared rhythm. The air was cool and pleasant, a mild breeze weaving through the trees and carrying the scent of earth warmed by the sun. Leaves rustled softly, and the distant hum of the river seemed to mingle with the murmurs of the devotees. They walked toward the food centre, where the aroma of South Indian dishes — tangy sambar, fragrant rice, crisp dosas, and spiced chutneys — mingled with the scent of the breeze, inviting both body and spirit to nourishment.

Meals shared in this way were more than sustenance. Each bite, each exchange, was an unspoken prayer — an offering of gratitude for the labour of those who had prepared the food, and for the company of those with whom it was shared. Conversation was gentle, laughter occasional, yet the energy of mindfulness pervaded every gesture.

After finishing, a few minutes of quiet reflection followed, and then Sam, Alice, Sofia, Bhavya, Aarna, Dev, and John gathered under the grand banyan tree. Its thick roots and sprawling canopy offered shade and a sense of ancient presence, a silent witness to countless gatherings like this. Soon, Akshaya, Padma, Vasudeva, Kiran, and Vidyarthi joined, followed by Aastha, Abhirami, and the others who had taken brief strolls to enjoy the sunlight and calm. Kieron, Astyn, Espen, Greta, and Divyani arrived, their presence carrying the quiet vitality of aligned breath and movement.

Nita, Lalitha, Rohith, and Sujitha joined next, and gradually the circle became whole as Abhilasha, Akanksh, Akshatha, Apeksha, and Roopa settled in. The group naturally fell into conversation, sharing reflections on the morning session — insights, questions, and small revelations interwoven like threads in a tapestry. The discussion was alive, yet gentle, each voice given space to rise and fall without hurry.

After a brief pause, Sofia's voice broke through the calm.

"Apeksha," she said softly, "please narrate a story."

The Silent Gardener

Long ago, in a village nestled between hills and rivers, there lived a gardener named Devak. His garden was humble, not the grand estate of the wealthy, but a small patch of earth he had tended for decades. Every morning, before the sun rose, he would kneel among the soil, speaking softly to the roots, thanking the earth for giving him life, nourishment, and purpose.

The villagers often passed by, curious. "Why do you speak to weeds?" they asked. "Why spend so long on flowers no one will notice?" Devak would smile quietly, saying nothing. He simply continued his work, pruning, watering, planting, and listening.

One season, a terrible drought struck the region. Crops withered, rivers receded, and villagers feared hunger. Yet Devak's small garden remained unexpectedly alive. When asked how he had survived, he only said, "I listen to the earth. I see what it needs and respond."

A traveller passing through asked him, "Surely this is mere chance?" Devak shook his head. "No," he said. "Every day, I honour what is here. The sun, the rain, the smallest leaf — I notice, I nurture, I am grateful. That is why life returns to me, even in hardship."

In time, the villagers began to see his garden differently. They realised that every flower, every sprout, every thriving root had grown from his patient acknowledgement, his silent gratitude for life itself. They began tending their own small gardens, offering thanks to the earth, to their neighbours, and to one another. Slowly, the entire village transformed — scarcity became creativity, division became collaboration, and complaint became reverence.

Devak, the silent gardener, never claimed credit. He never asked for recognition. Yet through simple acts of noticing, honouring, and nurturing life — even in ways unseen — he had sparked a ripple of transformation that extended far beyond the walls of his little garden.

Apeksha said, "Gratitude is not only in words. It is in noticing, in presence, in the care we offer silently. The world changes quietly, one unseen act at a time. What you tend in life — your awareness, your acknowledgment — blooms in ways you cannot yet imagine."

When her narration ended, a long silence followed. It was a silence full of weight and presence, the kind that occurs when a story has touched something unseen within each listener — a stillness that allowed the mind and heart to absorb, reflect, and integrate. The air felt alive, carrying the echoes of her words, as if the banyan itself held its breath in reverence.

Finally, Roopa exhaled softly, a mixture of reverence and readiness in her voice.

"It's time for Guruji's next session," she said, and the group slowly turned their attention back toward the hall, hearts quieted but alive, carrying the subtle transformation that comes when shared stories, presence, and reflection converge into a living experience.

The moment was both ending and beginning — the cycle of learning, awareness, and gratitude moving gently forward, as steady and natural as the river flowing through the village.

CHAPTER II

Gratitude and Nature

"Gratitude is not something to remember at day's end; it is a way of seeing each moment as it unfolds. The art of living is the art of noticing."

– Shree Shambav.

Synopsis

Nature is the original teacher of gratitude, offering lessons in abundance, impermanence, and interconnectedness. This chapter explores how attuning to the natural world cultivates awareness, humility, and reverence. From the gentle sway of trees to the roar of oceans, each element becomes a reflection of life's rhythms and a reminder of the gifts that surround us.

Gratitude for nature begins with presence—observing without judgment, listening without expectation, and feeling without interference. By recognising the cycles of growth, decay, and renewal, readers learn that everything in life flows in balance and that even endings carry seeds of new beginnings. Nature's resilience teaches acceptance, patience, and quiet joy, revealing that abundance is never external—it is a reflection of inner harmony.

Practical exercises include mindful walks, journaling inspired by natural phenomena, and daily acknowledgments of environmental beauty. The chapter also emphasises ecological gratitude, highlighting the importance of protecting and honouring the planet.

Ultimately, embracing gratitude in nature fosters deep emotional, spiritual, and psychological alignment. By seeing the sacred in trees, rivers, mountains, and sky, we reconnect to life itself, cultivating a sense of wonder, interconnectedness, and heartfelt appreciation that permeates all aspects of existence.

After a few moments of stillness, Guruji spoke, his voice soft and measured, carrying the warmth of the moment.

The Whisper of Trees – "Lessons in Stillness"

"Have you ever listened to a tree?" Guruji began. "Not just looked at it, but *listened*—beyond its rustle, beyond its sway?"

He paused, allowing the silence to deepen. "The tree," he continued, "is not merely a form. It is a silent teacher of patience, of surrender, of presence. Each branch holds the story of seasons—some broken by wind, some stretched toward the sun, and some carrying the weight of resting birds. Yet, through it all, the tree does not resist. It simply stands, deeply rooted, quietly alive."

The devotees listened intently, the breeze now playing softly through the banyan leaves, as though responding to his words.

Guruji continued, "When storms come, the tree bends; it does not fight. When drought arrives, it withdraws within, conserving its essence. And when spring returns, it does not boast—it simply blooms. In this rhythm lies life's secret. Gratitude grows in the same way—quietly, patiently, in harmony with what is. When we allow ourselves to bend instead of break, to observe instead of react, we begin to live with the grace of the tree."

He turned slightly, his gaze following the slow fall of a leaf as it drifted to the ground.

"Watch how it descends," he said softly. "It does not struggle. It dances its way back to the earth that once held it. Such is the way of life—everything returns, transformed, renewed. Gratitude is our awareness of this flow, of being part of something far greater than our individual desires or disappointments."

Alice spoke gently, "Guruji, sometimes it's difficult to stay still when life shakes us."

Guruji smiled, a knowing warmth in his eyes. "Yes," he said, "but stillness does not mean inaction. It is awareness in motion. The tree sways, yet it never forgets its roots. You may move, you may fall, you may even shed parts of yourself—but remain rooted in awareness. That root is your gratitude, your connection to life's essence."

He then drew a quiet analogy, his voice flowing like a stream through the still air. "When you sit beside a tree long enough, you will feel it breathing—not as air, but as presence. The same life that moves within it moves within you. The same patience, the same resilience, the same silent strength. That is why the ancients meditated under trees—not because trees are sacred, but because they awaken the sacred within us."

A hush fell over the group. The banyan leaves shimmered under the shifting sunlight, as though nodding in agreement.

Guruji said softly, his words sinking deep like roots seeking water. "The whisper of trees reminds us—life does not need to be forced. It unfolds in stillness, nourished by trust. Be like the tree—rooted in patience, open to the wind, grateful for both rain and sun. For in stillness, the heart learns to listen, and in listening, we remember who we are."

The devotees remained quiet; no one rushed to speak. Only the sound of wind through leaves filled the space — the whisper of trees carrying lessons older than words. In that silence, gratitude was not spoken; it was *felt* — vast, alive, and humbling.

Vidyarthi asked, "Guruji, when was the last time we truly listened to the voice of nature in silence — without distraction — and allowed its whispers to reveal their truth to us?"

Guruji looked at Vidyarthi with a soft, knowing smile — the kind that carried both silence and story within it. The hall grew still. Only the distant rustle of peepal leaves outside the open window filled the space, as if nature itself had paused to listen.

He said gently, "My child, most people walk through forests but never meet a single tree. They see the bark, the shape, the leaves — but they do not *listen.* To listen is not merely to hear sound, but to receive presence. Nature speaks in a language that cannot be written, only felt."

He closed his eyes for a moment and began to speak as though memory itself was unfolding:

There was once a traveller who lost his way in the mountains. The path that had once been clear vanished beneath a veil of fog and rain. His mind wrestled between fear and confusion — *Where do I go? How do I return?*

But as he paused beneath an ancient banyan tree, something subtle shifted. The rain began to soften. The mist grew luminous. The leaves, once trembling in chaos, now swayed with quiet rhythm — as if the forest itself had begun to breathe.

In that stillness, the traveller realised he was not lost. He was being held — not by the path beneath his feet, but by the presence around him. The tree stood tall in patient silence, unhurried by time. It had witnessed centuries of storms and sunlight, birds building homes and pilgrims seeking answers, yet it never asked for anything. It simply *was.*

That night, the traveller understood something profound: silence is not emptiness — it is communion. Stillness is not stagnation — it is surrender. The tree became a mirror, teaching through its unwavering presence that life speaks when we stop resisting it.

The whisper of the wind, the rhythm of falling rain, the pulse of the earth — all are gentle reminders that existence is never against us. It waits for us to pause, to breathe, and to listen. For when the noise within subsides, the voice of creation begins to speak.

Guruji opened his eyes. They shimmered with a quiet light.

He continued softly, "You see, Vidyarthi, nature doesn't shout like the world of men; it whispers. It doesn't instruct; it reveals. Each leaf turning to light, each breeze brushing your skin — they are reminders of the Divine breathing through creation.

When we listen deeply — truly listen — gratitude awakens not as a thought but as a pulse. We realise the same rhythm that moves through the river flows through our veins. The same stillness that holds the mountain also holds our mind.

That is when life becomes prayerful. Every tree becomes a teacher. Every breeze becomes a blessing."

He paused and looked toward the garden beyond the hall. The sunlight now danced upon the neem leaves, and the faint fragrance of earth filled the air after a recent drizzle.

"Go," he said softly. "Sit beneath a tree today. Not to meditate, not to seek, not even to thank — but simply to *listen.* Let the silence between the rustling leaves tell you the story of patience. Let the wind remind you that surrender is not weakness — it is rhythm.

Then you will understand: nature doesn't ask for gratitude; it teaches us how to live it."

The Flow of Water – "Life's Unseen Currents."

Guruji said, Water has always been life's silent teacher. It flows without argument, without expectation. It does not resist the stone that blocks its path, nor does it cling to the shore that once embraced it. Instead, it finds a way — sometimes by slipping gently around, sometimes by carving through, and sometimes by resting until the obstacle itself erodes.

Life, too, moves in unseen currents. Sometimes it carries us with ease, and sometimes it drags us into turbulence where we can no longer see the shore. Yet, even in chaos, there is intelligence — a rhythm deeper than control, a wisdom older than fear. Gratitude is what allows us to trust that rhythm.

Guruji paused, then spoke softly, "Let me tell you a story."

In a small mountain village, there lived a potter named Amara. Every day, she fetched water from a nearby stream that wound its way through rocks and roots before reaching the valley. One summer, the rains failed, and the stream thinned into trickles. Villagers grumbled in despair, fearing their crops would die. But Amara continued to visit the stream daily. She would sit by its edge, fill her half-empty pot, and whisper a silent thank you.

One morning, as she sat by the dry bed, an elder passing by asked, "Why thank a stream that gives you so little?"

Amara smiled. "Because it still flows," she said. "It reminds me that even when life slows, it hasn't stopped. The flow may be hidden beneath the soil, but it's there — carrying what's needed where it's needed."

Weeks later, when the monsoon finally came, the same stream overflowed, bringing freshness and life to the valley once more. But Amara's heart was already full — not because the waters returned, but because she had learned to trust the unseen flow that never truly left.

Guruji looked at his devotees and said, "Gratitude is not born from abundance — it *creates* abundance. When we stop resisting life's changing tides, we discover that everything we need is already flowing toward us. The current of existence never ceases; only our perception of lack blinds us to it."

He continued, "To live like water is to accept impermanence not as loss, but as renewal. The river that leaves the mountain does not mourn the snow it once was — it celebrates its transformation. Likewise, gratitude turns every ending into a beginning, every letting go into a greater arrival."

The hall was silent. Outside, a gentle drizzle began. It was as though nature itself had bowed in agreement — whispering its eternal lesson: **Flow, don't fight. Trust, don't grasp. Be grateful, and the current of life will always carry you home.**

Aastha asked, "Guruji, how can we learn to let life flow in its natural rhythm — embracing even the unforeseen currents with a heart of gratitude?"

Guruji smiled at Aastha's question — one that lingered in the air like the faint echo of temple bells after prayer. His eyes reflected both compassion and a knowing stillness, as though the answer was not something to be found in words but felt in the rhythm between them.

He said softly, "Aastha, to let life flow in its natural rhythm is to trust the intelligence of existence itself. Just as the river does not ask where it is going, yet always finds its way to the sea, we too must learn to surrender to the deeper current beneath our desires, fears, and expectations."

He paused, letting the silence stretch like a gentle breath. "But surrender," he continued, "is not passive. It is a living trust — a cooperation with the unseen. When you resist the current, life becomes a struggle. When you flow with it, even pain carries wisdom."

The Story of the Potter's River

Once, in a serene valley nestled between mountains, lived a young potter named Leela. She crafted her pots by the river that ran beside her hut. The river was her constant companion — sometimes fierce, sometimes tender — always teaching her through its moods.

One year, a heavy storm struck the valley. The river flooded, sweeping away her small kiln and the pots she had made for the annual market. Her heart broke; months of work vanished overnight. She sat by the riverbank for days, weeping at its cruelty. "Why would you destroy me," she whispered, "when I have loved you all my life?"

The river, of course, gave no reply. But in the days that followed, Leela noticed something strange. The floodwaters had unearthed a bed of fine clay — softer and purer than any she had ever used before. Slowly, she began again, shaping new pots, each one finer than the last. When she sold them in the market that year, her work caught the attention of a royal merchant, who offered her a place in the city's artisans' guild.

Standing once more by the river, she bowed and said, "What I thought was destruction was your way of renewal."

Guruji looked at Aastha. "That river is life, my dear. Sometimes it washes away what we cling to, not to punish us, but to make room for what we are meant to become. The clay of our destiny is revealed only when the old banks are broken."

He continued with quiet depth, "Gratitude is not merely saying *thank you* for what pleases us — it is the art of bowing even to what confuses or challenges us. When we embrace uncertainty, we align with the rhythm of the universe — like a dancer who no longer fights the music but becomes the movement itself."

Aastha lowered her gaze, her eyes moist. The gentle wind stirred through the trees, rustling the leaves in an unseen harmony. Guruji added, almost in a whisper,

"Remember, the river never rushes toward the sea in fear — it flows because it knows where it belongs. So must you. Gratitude transforms fear into flow, resistance into rhythm, and loss into liberation. Let life carry you, and you will never truly lose your way."

Light Beyond Measure

The devotees sat in quiet reverence as the soft glow of dusk filtered through the ashram courtyard. The breeze carried a faint fragrance of sandalwood and marigold. Guruji looked toward the horizon, where the sun had begun its slow descent, painting the sky in gold, rose, and indigo. His gaze was steady, as if reading a scripture written in light itself.

After a long, contemplative silence, Guruji spoke, his voice carrying both warmth and depth.

Guruji said, "The Sun and the Sky – *Light Beyond Measure*

"The sun," he began, "does not ask for gratitude, yet it gives endlessly. It rises without pride and sets without regret. It warms the seed, dries the tears of the earth, and paints the heavens with colours only silence can understand. And yet, how rarely do we pause to notice its gift.

We often measure our days by tasks and time—but the sun measures them by radiance and renewal. Its rising is a reminder that beginnings are possible, even after the longest night. Its setting teaches that even endings can be graceful, luminous, and full of promise."

He paused, letting the silence deepen. The air seemed to shimmer between his words.

"The sky," he continued, "receives everything—the storm, the sunlight, the drifting clouds, the cries of birds, and even our prayers. It holds both radiance and rain without judgment. Just as the sky holds the sun, life asks us to hold one another—with spaciousness, patience, and trust. Gratitude is born not only from receiving warmth but also from witnessing this vast embrace."

Guruji turned to the gathering. "The relationship between the sun and the sky is the purest reflection of divine love. The sun shines because it must, not for recognition. The sky receives because it can, not for possession. In their silent partnership lies the secret of gratitude — unconditional giving and graceful acceptance."

A still hush followed, until Sofia softly asked, "Guruji, how can we remember such vastness amid our small struggles?"

Guruji smiled gently. "By looking up," he said. "By remembering that our worries are like passing clouds, but our being — the awareness that watches — is the sky itself. And when you realise that the same light that touches the mountain also falls upon your face, gratitude is no longer a practice. It becomes your nature."

Then, as the evening deepened, he shared a story to anchor the truth in their hearts.

The Story of the Sky Painter

In a quiet coastal village lived an old painter named Arin. Each dawn, he would stand at the shore and gaze at the horizon, brush in hand, painting the sunrise on parchment. Villagers laughed gently at his ritual. "Why paint what the sky already paints?" they teased.

Arin would simply smile. "Because one day," he said, "I may forget to look."

Years passed. His paintings filled the walls of his small hut — no two alike, each capturing a hue the previous day had never known. Then one season, the rains came late. The villagers grew anxious. The sky remained grey and the sea restless. Arin, too, sat each morning with his brush, facing the clouded sky, waiting.

One evening, as the clouds broke open, the setting sun scattered crimson light across the water. Arin stood silently, tears glistening in his eyes. He did not lift his brush. He simply whispered, "Even when hidden, the sun never ceased to paint."

Guruji looked at his devotees, his eyes glowing softly in the twilight.

"Gratitude," he said, "is like Arin's faith. It is the remembrance that light exists even behind clouds. To thank the sun is to thank life itself — for shining, for hiding, for teaching us that what is unseen is often what sustains us most."

Abhirami's voice arose from that stillness, steady yet filled with wonder. "Guruji," she asked softly, "which aspect of nature awakens the deepest gratitude within us — the one that reminds us of life's boundless possibilities?"

Her question lingered, like a petal caught in midair. Guruji's eyes, half-closed, opened with quiet radiance.

Guruji spoke gently, "My child, nature is not separate from us — it is the mirror of our own soul. Each element holds a secret that can awaken the heart to gratitude. Yet if I were to name one, it would be *the horizon.*

The horizon is where the seen and unseen meet — where the known world bows to mystery. Every dawn it reminds us that light will always return, and every dusk it teaches that endings, too, are promises of renewal. To gaze at the horizon is to remember that life is not a straight line, but an eternal meeting between what we know and what we have yet to become."

He looked toward the distance, where the sun had begun its descent, touching the treetops with a molten glow.

"The horizon," he continued, "is neither earth nor sky. It belongs to both and to neither. It teaches us the art of belonging without possession — of embracing change without fear. Gratitude arises not from clinging to one form of beauty but from witnessing the endless ways beauty reveals itself. Just as the sun doesn't mourn the night, we too must learn to trust life's turning seasons.

When we learn to live like the horizon — grounded like the earth, yet open as the sky — we become vessels of grace. Gratitude then is not something we express; it becomes the way we breathe."

The devotees listened, their eyes glistening with reflection. A hush settled until Aarna whispered, "Guruji… it's as if the horizon holds the breath of God."

Guruji smiled, his expression serene. "Yes," he said softly, "and every morning, that breath becomes visible again. The world bows to it, and so should we."

He paused, then continued with a story that carried the essence of that truth.

The Horizon Keeper

Once, in a coastal village, there lived an old woman named Chinmayee who was known as *The Horizon Keeper*. Each morning before dawn, she would walk barefoot to the edge of the sea and light a small lamp. No one knew why she did this. Children would follow her, curious, whispering, "Is she calling the sun?"

One day, a traveller asked her, "Why do you light this lamp, Mother? The sun rises on its own."

Chinmayee smiled, her eyes reflecting the rippling sea. "Yes," she said, "the sun does not need my lamp. But need to remember its coming. My lamp is my gratitude — not for what I see, but for what I trust will arrive."

Years passed, and the villagers grew accustomed to the sight of her small flame flickering against the vast dawn. When Chinmayee passed away, the villagers began lighting their own lamps each morning at the shore. Over time, the coast became known as *The Bay of Lights*. Travellers who arrived there at sunrise would see dozens of small flames shimmering across the horizon — like stars waiting to be reborn.

Guruji looked at his devotees, his voice low and tender.

"Chinmayee's lamp is the light of remembrance — the acknowledgement that every day is a gift, not a guarantee. The horizon holds the promise that even when we cannot see what lies ahead, something greater is always unfolding."

He paused, and the devotees felt as though the horizon itself had drawn nearer — as if the sky leaned in to listen.

"Gratitude," Guruji said, "is the lamp we light within — not to summon the sun, but to honour its eternal return."

Gratitude for the World

Guruji said, "Gratitude for the World – Stewardship and Sacredness"

"Gratitude," he said, "is more than feeling thankful for what we receive. True gratitude blossoms when it moves into action. The world does not ask for praise; it asks for care. Every river, every tree, every breath of wind is a gift, and to honour it is not only reverence — it is responsibility."

He let the words settle, then continued: "Consider the forest. It does not keep a ledger of what it gives or receives. It simply exists, in a delicate balance, sustaining life in countless unseen ways. And yet, it can be harmed — by neglect, by thoughtless use, by forgetting its sacredness. When we honour the earth, we acknowledge that we are part of this rhythm, not separate from it. Gratitude is realised through stewardship, through mindful action."

The Fisherman and the Tide

In a small coastal village, a fisherman named Tavin rose each morning before dawn, his hands calloused from years of work, his heart attuned to the rhythm of the sea. Generations of his family had lived by the bounty of these waters, and Tavin knew its moods intimately — the days when the tide was generous, and the days when it withheld its gifts.

Yet that year, the catch began to dwindle. Nets came up nearly empty. The villagers grew anxious, voices rising in blame — the river, the weather, even one another. Fear and frustration hung over the village like a fog.

Tavin, however, did not speak hastily. He watched the currents, the shoreline, and the patterns of life around him. Slowly, he noticed the signs: trash swept in by the waves, discarded nets snagging rocks, and mangroves felled to make way for new huts. The sea had not turned against them — they had turned against the delicate balance that sustained it.

With quiet determination, Tavin began small, deliberate acts of care. Each morning, he cleared debris from the shore. He nurtured the young mangrove saplings, protecting them from harm. When tiny fish became trapped in his nets, he carefully returned them to the water. Day by day, these small gestures rippled through the ecosystem.

Gradually, the tides began to shift. Nets once again filled with fish. The river hummed with renewed life. But the greatest change was in the villagers themselves. They saw the sea no longer as a mere resource to be taken, but as a living partner — one that required respect, attentiveness, and gratitude expressed through care, not words.

Tavin's lesson was simple yet profound: when we honour the balance of life, the world responds. Gratitude is not only felt; it is lived. And in that living, both giver and gift are transformed.

Guruji looked at the devotees, "Like Tavin, we must learn to treat the world as sacred. Gratitude is not only in recognition; it is in action. The soil, the rivers, the forests, the animals — all are reflections of the same life force that flows through you. When you protect and nurture them, gratitude multiplies. Your heart and the world's heart beat in rhythm."

He continued, "Each mindful choice — planting a tree, cleaning a stream, using resources wisely — is a prayer of thankfulness. Every act of care becomes a bridge between yourself and the sacredness surrounding you. To honour the earth is to honour life itself, and to honour life is to awaken the deepest, most sustaining form of gratitude."

The group fell silent, listening to the soft rustle of leaves, the distant call of a bird, the subtle pulse of the world around them. For a moment, every breath seemed intertwined with the earth's, and gratitude was no longer a thought — it was a living, breathing presence.

Sam's voice broke the serene rhythm, gentle but earnest.

"Guruji," he asked, "what simple acts can we embody each day to honour and give back to the natural world that sustains us?"

The question hovered in the air, carrying the weight of sincere curiosity and the unspoken longing to align action with awareness. Guruji's gaze drifted over the gathering, then rested on the horizon where the sun kissed the earth. His voice, calm yet luminous, unfolded like the rhythm of a river:

Guruji said, "Acts of Gratitude in Daily Life – The Dance of Reciprocity"

"Sam," he began, "gratitude toward the natural world is not measured in grand gestures. It is in the small, conscious acts performed with awareness. Each action is a note in the symphony of reciprocity. A single seed planted, water offered to a thirsty plant, a path cleared of litter, or mindful use of resources — these are not trivial. They are prayers in motion.

"Consider the river," he continued. "It flows endlessly, giving without thought of return. We, too, can mirror this generosity in tiny, intentional ways. Sweep the fallen leaves into nourishment for the soil, offer scraps to the birds or the earth, and choose what you consume with care. These actions ripple outward, unseen, like currents beneath the surface, eventually returning blessings greater than we imagine."

The Lantern Maker and the Grove

In a quiet village bordered by hills and forests, there lived a lantern maker named Ishan. His lanterns were sought far and wide for their delicate craftsmanship and the soft, steady glow they emitted. One evening, while collecting materials in the forest, he noticed a small grove of saplings, wilting under neglect. He could have walked on, thinking it was not his concern, but something inside him stirred.

Each day thereafter, Ishan tended the grove in small ways: watering the saplings, clearing weeds, protecting them from the curious animals of the night. As he worked, he noticed the forest respond — leaves seemed greener, the air fresher, and the birds more numerous. One morning, he realised that the grove's quiet revival mirrored something within himself: patience, care, and an inner light that grew in proportion to his service.

The villagers soon noticed Ishan's dedication. Inspired, they joined him, each contributing in their own way. Over time, the grove transformed into a sanctuary, a living testament to gratitude in action. The lanterns he crafted now carried not just light, but the pulse of a world nurtured by conscious care.

Guruji looked around the circle, his voice soft but unwavering:

"Sam, this is the essence of daily stewardship. You do not need to save the world in one grand act. Begin where you stand, with what is closest to you. Plant, water, protect, and notice. Gratitude manifests most vividly when paired with care. Each small gesture echoes through the web of life, unseen yet infinitely potent.

"When we honour the natural world in these ways, we recognise that we are not separate from it. We are threads woven into its tapestry. And in honouring it, we honour ourselves — our own breath, our own light, our own sacred connection to all that sustains us."

Guruji's gaze drifted toward the horizon, and after a reflective pause, he spoke with a calm warmth that seemed to touch each heart.

"Let me narrate a story," he said, his voice carrying the cadence of contemplation.

The Old Oak and the Wanderer

Once, a wanderer, weary from long journeys through mountains, valleys, and villages, stumbled upon a vast oak tree in the middle of a sunlit meadow. Its trunk was wide and gnarled, its branches reaching high as though embracing the sky itself. The wanderer paused beneath its shade, drawn not by thirst or hunger, but by a quiet sense of welcome.

As he sat, he felt the wind whisper through the leaves, each gust carrying stories of storms weathered, seasons endured, and quiet growth. Birds perched in the branches, insects hummed along the roots, and the grass swayed rhythmically — a symphony of life unnoticed yet unwavering.

For hours, the wanderer observed. He watched the resilience of life around him — how even in harsh sun or sudden storm, each creature and leaf found its balance. Slowly, his thoughts turned inward. He saw his own struggles mirrored in the oak's enduring presence: losses he had carried, fears he had battled, and joys he had overlooked. He understood, with sudden clarity, that like the oak, resilience is silent, gratitude is quiet, and true strength is rooted deeply, often unseen.

Rising at last to continue his journey, the wanderer bowed his head in reverence beneath the ancient branches and whispered, "Thank you for holding me, for teaching me to bend without breaking, and for reminding me that life, in all its forms, is sacred."

From that day forward, he carried the oak's lesson wherever he went. In every encounter, in every hardship and small delight, he remembered to see, to honour, and to feel gratitude in every living moment — knowing that the sacredness of the world outside mirrors the sacredness within.

Guruji looked at the devotees with a soft smile in his eyes. "The oak does not ask for thanks, nor does it demand recognition. Yet its presence teaches the heart to notice, to respect, and to respond with reverence. Gratitude begins with awareness — the recognition that the world itself is a living teacher, offering lessons in patience, endurance, and sacredness at every step."

The group remained in silent reflection, feeling the depth of the lesson settle like sunlight in their hearts, each aware that the world — like the old oak — held them in quiet, steadfast grace.

After a long pause, Guruji spoke, his voice calm and warm, "Let us take an evening break."

One by one, the devotees rose and slowly walked out of Buddha Hall. The courtyard was bathed in the soft glow of twilight. A cool breeze meandered through the air, carrying the heady fragrance of jasmine and other night-blooming flowers. The sun had begun its descent, painting the horizon in shades of amber and rose, while birds returned to their nests, their calls fading into the approaching stillness. Darkness crept softly over the edges of the garden, and the first stars began to appear, faint but steady, like tiny reminders of constancy in a changing world.

Sam, Alice, Sofia, Bhavya, Aarna, Dev, and John gathered beneath the sprawling banyan tree. Soon, Akshaya, Padma, Vasudeva, Kiran, and Vidyarthi joined them after a brief stroll through the temple gardens. Aastha and Abhirami followed, their laughter quiet, mingling with the gentle rustle of leaves. Before long, Kieron, Astyn, Espen, Greta, and Divyani joined the circle, carrying the warmth of the day's walk into the shared space of conversation.

From the edge of the courtyard, Abhilasha, Akanksh, Akshatha, and Apeksha approached, trays in hand, bearing coffee, herbal tea, and delicate cookies. The aroma of fresh brew mingled with the jasmine-scented breeze, creating a sense of comfort and homeliness. Each devotee accepted the offerings with gratitude, feeling the subtle warmth not just from the cups in their hands but from the presence of community and shared stillness.

Sofia lifted her cup of herbal tea, letting the steam curl upward like a whispered prayer. She turned to Apeksha and said softly, "Apeksha, please narrate a story."

The Lantern Keeper and the Misty Lake

Apeksha's voice rose softly, weaving through the twilight air, "Long ago, in a village tucked between hills and a misty lake, there lived an old lantern keeper named Arin. Each evening, he would light lanterns along the shore, their warm glow dancing across the water. Travellers often asked him, 'Why do you bother? The mist will cover them anyway.'

Arin would smile, his eyes reflecting the flickering lights. 'The lanterns are not for the mist,' he said. 'They are for the ones who walk with uncertainty, so they may find their way. And sometimes… they remind even the keeper of the path home.'

One year, the lake swelled beyond its banks after an unusually heavy monsoon. Paths disappeared beneath rising water, and the villagers feared the worst. The lanterns, once small beacons along familiar trails, now seemed like tiny sparks against the vastness of the flood.

Arin did not despair. Night after night, he carried his lanterns along the lake's edge, placing them where the water touched the trees, where the reeds swayed like dancers, and where the fog pressed thickest. Slowly, villagers who had been lost in worry and fear noticed the soft light guiding them — they walked safely, finding their way home.

When the floods receded, they gathered around Arin and said, 'Your small lights saved us. We were afraid we could do nothing.' Arin shook his head gently. 'The light does not save,' he said. 'It only reveals what was always there. The courage, the care, and the path were within you all along.'

From that day, the villagers no longer saw lanterns as mere lights — they saw them as reminders of the unseen currents of life: patience, presence, and quiet care. And Arin, the keeper of lanterns, continued his walk each evening, not to control the mist or the water, but to honour it, and in doing so, he discovered that gratitude, like light, spreads quietly but endlessly."

The circle fell silent. Even the breeze seemed to pause as the last note of Apeksha's voice faded. Each devotee felt the lesson in their heart: that small, mindful acts of care illuminate the world in ways no one may see, and gratitude is expressed not in words alone, but in the quiet tending of life itself.

After a few minutes, Abhilasha, sensing the natural pause had reached its close, spoke gently, "Time for Guruji's next session."

The group rose slowly, carrying with them the quiet illumination of the evening — the lingering lessons of the story, the shared warmth of tea and companionship, and the delicate wonder of twilight blending into night.

CHAPTER III

Gratitude as a Daily Practice

"What connects us to each other, to nature, and to life itself is unseen — a thread woven of compassion, humility, and grace. Gratitude is what keeps it from breaking."

– Shree Shambav.

Synopsis

Gratitude is most powerful when it evolves from occasional reflection into a daily, intentional practice. This chapter explores how consistent acknowledgement of life's gifts rewires the mind, transforms perception, and elevates emotional well-being. Readers learn that gratitude is not merely a response to abundance, but a discipline that uncovers richness in every moment—even in the mundane or difficult.

Daily gratitude strengthens awareness, cultivates resilience, and nurtures joy. The chapter provides practical methods: morning reflections, journaling prompts, mindful pauses, gratitude letters, and evening recaps. These practices embed thankfulness into thought patterns, gradually reshaping reactions to stress, disappointment, and uncertainty.

The chapter also emphasises the integration of gratitude into relationships, work, and personal growth. By consciously appreciating others, celebrating progress, and acknowledging small victories, readers create a ripple effect that fosters positivity in all spheres of life.

Ultimately, this chapter positions gratitude as a lifestyle—a choice, a habit, and a guiding principle. When gratitude becomes a daily practice, it transforms perception, deepens connection, and unlocks inner peace. The final lessons encourage readers to carry the art of gratitude forward, making it a compass for navigating life's challenges and joys with grace, awareness, and love.

Guruji said, "Morning Reflections – Starting the Day with Thanks"

Guruji said softly, "A simple practice of recognising what you are grateful for upon waking sets the tone, focus, and energy for the day. Gratitude begins before the mind awakens to the world's demands, before the noise of thought drowns the silence of being."

He paused, allowing his words to settle like dew upon their hearts.

"The mind," he continued, "is often like an untuned instrument. It wakes restless, already anticipating what must be done, who must be pleased, what must be achieved. But when we pause—just for a moment—before touching the world, and whisper a quiet *thank you*, we tune ourselves to harmony. That single act, invisible to others, aligns us with the rhythm of creation."

Guruji said, "When the sun rises, it does not ask if the world deserves its light—it simply gives. In the same way, gratitude does not wait for perfect circumstances. It simply notices what *is*—the breath, the warmth of life, the quiet heartbeat of existence. Gratitude is the soul's first prayer, offered even before words are spoken."

Guruji's eyes softened. "Each morning is a rebirth, a chance to begin again. If the first thought of the day is gratitude, the rest of the day becomes a reflection of that grace."

The Story of the Potter's Dawn

In a quiet village by the river, there lived a potter named Devraj. Each morning, before the sun rose, he would sit beside his wheel, eyes closed, palms resting on the cool clay. He would whisper, *"Thank you for the earth beneath my hands."*

The villagers often mocked his ritual. "Why, thank the clay?" they asked. "It is you who shapes it!"

Devraj only smiled. "I shape the clay, yes," he said, "but it is the earth that gives it form, the water that softens it, the fire that strengthens it, and the air that cools it. I only cooperate."

Years passed. One morning, a storm flooded the village, washing away many homes, including Devraj's workshop. When the storm subsided, the villagers found him sitting beside the ruins—calm, unmoving, his hands again resting on the mud.

"Are you not broken?" they asked.

He replied, "How can I be broken by the very earth that holds me? It has given me everything—and now, it asks me to begin again."

And with that, he began shaping a small clay lamp, right there amidst the wreckage.

Guruji's voice softened, almost blending with the rustle of the trees outside.

"Each morning, like Devraj, we are given new clay—the raw material of another day. It may be smooth or rough, wet or dry, easy or challenging. But how we touch it, how we shape it, depends on the hands of our awareness. Gratitude is not for what we hold—it is for the chance to hold it at all."

He looked at the gathering of devotees, each lost in their own silence, and concluded gently,

"When you wake tomorrow, do not rush to remember what you must do. Remember first that you are here—that life has chosen you once more to see, to love, to learn, to create. That is the first gift of the day. Honour it. The world awakens through your gratitude."

Akshaya asked, "Guruji, what three things can we consciously acknowledge each morning to anchor our day in gratitude and inner harmony?"

Akshaya's question lingered in the air — gentle yet profound.

Guruji closed his eyes for a moment, as though listening not to the question, but to the silence behind it. When he finally spoke, his voice was calm and filled with the warmth of deep knowing.

Guruji said, "Each morning, before the noise of the world enters your mind, you can awaken your spirit through three sacred recognitions — three anchors that align your heart, body, and soul with the rhythm of life.

First, recognise the gift of breath.

The very act of breathing is the first miracle of the day. When you wake, the breath that greets you is not yours to command — it is life's way of saying, *'You are still part of this unfolding creation.'*

Pause and breathe consciously. Feel the air enter your lungs, filling you with existence itself. Gratitude for breath reminds you that before any success, task, or identity, you are a living expression of life's generosity.

Second, recognise the presence of those who sustain you.

Think of the people, seen and unseen, who shape your life — your family, friends, the farmers who grew your food, the unseen hands who bring light, water, and comfort into your world. Gratitude for them transforms isolation into connection. It softens the ego's illusion that you stand alone. Each morning, when you thank even one being — human, animal, or divine — you align with the web of interdependence that sustains creation.

Third, recognise your purpose for the day.

Ask your heart, *'How can I serve today? How can I add a little more light?'* This doesn't mean grand gestures. It could be a smile, a kind word, or patience when the world tests you. Gratitude becomes action when it flows through your choices. A grateful heart doesn't merely receive; it radiates. Purpose gives your gratitude direction, turning awareness into harmony."

Guruji paused. The soft sound of a cuckoo echoed from the nearby grove. The devotees sat still — even the wind seemed to hold its breath.

He continued gently, "When you begin your day with these three recognitions — **breath, connection, and purpose** — your inner compass steadies. The day no longer feels like a race to be run, but a melody to be played with grace. Gratitude in the morning is not about listing blessings; it is about tuning your being to the right frequency — the frequency of presence."

"Just as the lotus opens only in the light," Guruji said softly, "so too the heart opens only in gratitude. Begin your mornings not with haste, but with remembrance — remembrance that life itself is a divine invitation to love, to serve, and to be."

Padma whispered, "Guruji, it feels as if every breath now has meaning."

Guruji smiled. "That is the essence of morning reflection, my child — to awaken *before* the day begins, not just in body, but in spirit."

The devotees bowed their heads in silence. The morning had turned brighter, not just in light, but in awareness — as if gratitude itself had dawned upon their hearts.

Journaling and Mindful Pauses

Guruji closed his eyes for a brief moment, as if listening to something only silence could reveal. Then, with a soft yet luminous tone, he said, "When we write, we do not merely record — we *return*," Guruji began. "Each word becomes a mirror reflecting what we might otherwise overlook. Gratitude, when written, ceases to be a fleeting emotion and becomes a living imprint of awareness."

He paused, letting his gaze drift toward the dimly lit courtyard beyond Buddha Hall. The flame of the *jyoti* flickered in the distance, its soft glow dancing in rhythm with the evening wind.

"Most people," he continued, "rush through their days as though gratitude were waiting at the finish line — something to be felt after success, after peace, after everything aligns. But journaling changes that. It reminds us that the sacred is not found in grand achievements, but in noticing what is *already here*."

Guruji leaned slightly forward, his voice gentle yet resonant, like a stream gliding over smooth stones. "Let me tell you a story," he said.

The Story of the Lantern Maker

In a small town near the mountains lived a lantern maker named Elian. Every evening, he would light hundreds of lamps that illuminated the village streets.

People admired his work, yet Elian was not known for his craft alone — he was known for his calm presence, his unhurried way of being.

One night, a traveller stopped by his shop and asked, "Old man, how do you stay so peaceful in a world that is always rushing?"

Elian smiled and replied, "Each night, after the last lamp is lit, I write down three lights that I could not see during the day."

The traveller looked puzzled. "Three lights?"

"Yes," said Elian. "One light from what went well, one from what challenged me, and one from what I took for granted. I write them down — not for remembrance, but for revelation."

The traveller asked, "And what do you gain from that?"

Elian looked at the glow of the nearest lantern and whispered, "When I pause and write, I see how many lights I had missed in my haste. The act of seeing them — truly seeing — turns ordinary living into sacred dwelling."

Guruji smiled faintly as he finished the story. "You see," he said softly, "the written word carries energy. When you pen down your gratitude, your awareness deepens — your neural patterns align with harmony, not lack. A pause between thoughts becomes a bridge between the seen and unseen. That bridge is mindfulness."

He looked around at his devotees — Apeksha, Abhilasha, Akshaya, Kiran, Sofia — their eyes reflecting the lamplight and quiet reverence. "Do not let the day slip into night unnoticed," Guruji said finally. "Pause. Reflect. Write. Even a single line of awareness can illuminate what the rushing mind forgets to honour."

Outside, the night deepened — crickets sang in rhythm, the fragrance of jasmine lingered, and the soft hum of life continued under the watchful stillness of the stars.

And somewhere in that silence, each devotee resolved to carry a lantern within — lit not by oil or flame, but by the gentle light of awareness.

Capturing the Moment

Padma asked, "Guruji, how can journaling or mindful pauses help us awaken deeper appreciation for the beauty hidden in ordinary moments?"

Guruji smiled softly as Padma's question settled into the quiet of the hall. The night outside was deep and serene, and a cool breeze carried the faint fragrance of jasmine through the open windows. The devotees sat in a gentle half-circle, the golden light of the *jyoti* flickering between them.

Guruji looked at Padma and said, "Your question, my child, touches the essence of awareness. Beauty is never absent — it is merely unseen when the mind rushes. The art of journaling and mindful pauses is the art of *slowing down enough to see again.*"

He paused, his eyes resting on the flame before him. "Life hides its wonders not because it wishes to withhold them, but because our gaze often passes too quickly. When you stop, breathe, and write, you begin to untangle perception from hurry. You invite awareness back home."

He then said, "Let me share with you a story."

The Story of the Gardener and the Seeds

Once there was a gardener named Zoya who loved flowers but had grown weary of tending them. Seasons passed, yet her blooms were sparse, her soil dry, and her heart restless. One morning, she decided to leave her garden behind and travel to the nearby hills to seek inspiration.

After days of wandering, she met an old monk sitting under a flowering tree. Curious, she asked him,

“Master, why does this tree bloom so fully while my garden struggles to survive?”

The monk smiled and handed her a small pouch of seeds. “These are not ordinary seeds,” he said. “They bloom when planted with *attention.* Each day, give them not just water, but your *presence.*”

Zoya returned home, sceptical yet curious. She prepared the soil and planted the seeds. But this time, instead of rushing through her work, she began to pause. She watched how the morning dew formed on the leaves, how the ants carried crumbs, how the sunlight danced through the branches. She began writing these small wonders in a journal — not as a record, but as a way of seeing.

Days turned into weeks. The garden slowly transformed. Flowers bloomed with colours she had never seen before. And as her garden awakened, so did her heart. She realised it was not the soil that had been barren — it was her *attention* that had dried up.

One evening, as the sun painted the sky with shades of gold, Zoya wrote in her journal: “Beauty was never lost. I was simply too hurried to notice.”

Guruji looked up from his stillness, his voice a gentle stream flowing through the silence.

“When we journal,” he said, “we are not merely writing about life — we are *listening* to it. The act of recording deepens the experience. It teaches the mind to notice — the curve of a leaf, the warmth of sunlight, the taste of simple food, the presence of breath itself."

He turned his gaze to Padma. "A mindful pause is like the gardener's breath between each act of care. It allows you to feel the sacred pulse of ordinary existence. When you pause, the mundane reveals its hidden divinity. That is when gratitude blossoms — not as thought, but as *being.*"

He closed his eyes briefly, as if communing with something beyond words.

"Journaling," he concluded softly, "is the mirror that reflects your inner garden. Each word is a seed. And every moment you pause to write, you water the soil of awareness. Over time, what grows is not merely gratitude — it is reverence."

Outside, the moon had risen fully. Its silver light fell upon the quiet trees, the still pond, and the soft faces of the devotees who sat in awe — realising that the beauty they sought in life had always been right before them, waiting to be *seen.*

Gratitude in Relationships

The soft glow of the *jyoti* flickered in rhythmic harmony with the rustle of the wind outside. The fragrance of sandalwood lingered in the Buddha Hall, and the devotees sat in still reverence, their minds open, hearts receptive. Guruji's eyes glimmered in the dim light, calm yet luminous — like a lake reflecting the moon.

After a long pause, he said in a low, resonant voice, "Gratitude in relationships is the purest mirror of the soul's maturity. It is not merely about saying *thank you*; it is about *seeing* the other — truly seeing — beyond their actions, flaws, and masks. Gratitude is the bridge that connects two hearts, reminding each that love thrives not in perfection, but in recognition."

He smiled gently and continued, "Let me share a story."

The Lantern Maker and the Child

In a small riverside town, there lived an old lantern maker named Rohan. His hands were worn and wrinkled, yet every lantern he crafted glowed with extraordinary warmth. Each evening, people would buy his lanterns to light their homes and celebrate festivals, but few ever stopped to notice the man behind the light.

One day, a little girl named Kareena wandered into his shop. Her eyes sparkled with curiosity as she watched him bend thin strips of bamboo, glue the paper, and carefully paint soft patterns of stars and moons.

"Why do you make so many lanterns, Baba?" she asked.
Rohan smiled, "Because light deserves to travel, my child. Even if it begins in small hands."

The girl visited him every evening after school. Sometimes she would hand him brushes; other times, she'd listen to his quiet stories about the moon, the rivers, and the light that lives within every soul.

Seasons changed. Festivals came and went. Rohan grew older, his hands trembling, his eyes dim. The townspeople began buying lanterns from other shops — faster, cheaper, brighter. The old man's little workshop stood mostly empty.

One evening, Kareena returned, now grown into a young woman. She found Rohan sitting by the riverbank, a single unlit lantern beside him. Without a word, she knelt and lit it. The warm glow illuminated his tired face.

"Baba," she said softly, "your light still shines in every home I pass. You taught me what it means to give without expecting. You made me see that gratitude is the true flame that never dies."

Tears glistened in the lantern maker's eyes. For the first time, he realised that the countless lanterns he had made had not gone unseen. His light had been carried forward — through a child's heart, through remembrance, through gratitude.

That night, the river reflected hundreds of lights as Kareena and the villagers lit lanterns in his honour. Rohan passed away peacefully, his face calm, illuminated by the glow of countless thank-yous that had finally returned to him.

When the story ended, silence filled the hall. Guruji's voice broke the stillness, gentle yet profound: "Relationships are like lanterns. Each acknowledgement is a flame — fragile yet powerful. When we express gratitude, we give warmth, not just to others, but to ourselves. We remind one another that we are seen, valued, and connected."

He looked at his devotees and continued, "When gratitude is absent, even love feels unseen. But when gratitude flows, even silence speaks affection. It's not the grand gestures that sustain bonds; it's the quiet recognition — the 'I see you,' the 'thank you,' the 'I remember your effort' — that nurtures the invisible threads between souls."

Guruji leaned back, eyes half-closed, as if listening to the unspoken harmony among them. "When we mirror appreciation," he said finally, "we reflect the divine light that exists in all beings. Just as the lantern carries fire within paper and bamboo, so too our relationships carry sacredness within vulnerability. Gratitude doesn't just illuminate the path — it *becomes* the light."

Outside, a night breeze rustled through the trees, and somewhere in the distance, a temple bell echoed softly. The devotees sat in silence — each heart glowing like a small lantern, newly aware of the sacredness that lived quietly in every connection they had ever known.

The Mirror of Appreciation

Vasudeva asked, "Guruji, who in our life deserves our heartfelt recognition today, and how might we express our appreciation in a way that truly touches their soul?"

The question lingered in the quiet hall like the fading echo of a temple bell.

Vasudeva's voice was soft, almost reflective, yet it carried a depth that made everyone turn inward.

Guruji sat still for a moment, his eyes lowered, fingers lightly touching the beads of his mala. The gentle flame of the *jyoti* flickered beside him, casting warm shadows across his serene face. After a long silence, he looked up — not at Vasudeva, but as if he were looking through time itself.

He began softly, his tone woven with tenderness and knowing:

"Vasudeva, there are those in our lives whose love is so steady, so quiet, that we stop noticing it — like the heartbeat we never hear but cannot live without. They are the unseen pillars who hold our days together — a mother who wakes early to prepare food before the world stirs, a friend who listens without seeking anything in return, a teacher who lights your path without asking for praise, or even a stranger whose one kind gesture eased your burden.

These souls do not demand recognition, but they deserve it most. For their giving is not loud — it is woven in the fabric of ordinary life. And gratitude, when expressed sincerely, has the power to awaken their spirit and our own."

He paused, eyes half-closed, and said, "Let me tell you a story."

The Musician and the Silent Listener

In a small town by the river, there lived a musician named Arin who played the flute every evening at the village square. His melodies were tender — they carried both sorrow and serenity, echoing through the streets like soft prayers.

Crowds gathered at first, applauding his talent. But as months passed, fewer people came. The world grew busier, and Arin's music became part of the background — unnoticed, unthanked.

Yet, one evening as he played by the river, he saw an old woman sitting on the far bank, still and silent, her eyes closed as if she were listening with her heart. She came again the next day, and the next, never missing an evening, never saying a word.

Curious, Arin crossed the bridge one night and approached her.

"Mother," he asked gently, "why do you sit here listening every day? You never speak, yet you come without fail."

The old woman smiled faintly. "Your music," she said, "reminds me that my son's spirit is still near. He was a musician too. Since he passed, silence has been my home. But when you play, I remember love, not loss. I do not come to hear notes — I come to remember life."

Tears welled in Arin's eyes. That night, as he played, he no longer played *for* the crowd — he played *from* the heart. Each note became an offering, a bridge between souls.

Months later, when the old woman passed away, Arin found a small parchment near her resting place. On it were the words:

"Your music healed what time could not. Thank you for being the echo of love I once knew."

From that day forward, Arin began every performance by bowing to the river, whispering a silent prayer of gratitude — for the listener who taught him that appreciation is not applause, but presence.

Guruji's eyes softened as he finished the story. He let the silence settle before speaking again.

"You see, Vasudeva," he said gently, "those who deserve our recognition are not always the ones who seek it. They are the quiet givers, the silent healers, the gentle lights in the background of our lives. When we take a moment to see them — truly see them — and express gratitude with sincerity, we awaken something sacred within both hearts."

He continued with a slow, reflective cadence:

"Words alone do not touch the soul; it is the presence behind the words that does. A letter written from the heart, a gaze that says *thank you without speech*, a touch that acknowledges unseen effort — these are the true offerings of the grateful heart."

The devotees sat deeply still. The night was thick with quiet thought; even the wind seemed to listen. The lamp flame quivered softly, casting moving patterns on the floor — like the ripples of unseen gratitude moving through the room.

Guruji's voice dropped to a whisper, yet carried immense weight: "When you recognise another's light, you strengthen your own. When you honour the giver, you become one. Gratitude expressed sincerely is not flattery — it is *prayer made visible*."

He looked toward Vasudeva and said finally, "So tonight, before you rest, think of one person who silently gives to your life — perhaps someone you have overlooked. Offer them your appreciation — not as duty, but as devotion. Let them know they are seen. That single act, my dear ones, can turn an ordinary life into a sacred connection."

The hall remained in silence.

Outside, the night sky shimmered with faint starlight, as if the universe itself was echoing Guruji's words: *"When we give thanks to those who sustain us, we become part of the eternal music that holds the world together."*

Recaps and Reflection

The lamps flickered softly in the Buddha Hall. The air was cool and fragrant with sandalwood and the faint sweetness of jasmine drifting through the open windows. The devotees sat in stillness, their faces illuminated by the golden glow of the *jyoti*. Outside, the night sky shimmered with distant stars — quiet witnesses to another day's unfolding.

Guruji's gaze lingered on the flame for a moment before he spoke. His voice was calm, low, and filled with warmth — like the final note of a hymn before silence takes over.

"Evening is a sacred hour," Guruji said. "It is the bridge between what was lived and what is to come. We rush to begin the day, but rarely do we pause to close it — to gather its meaning, its blessings, its lessons."

He looked around, meeting the eyes of his devotees. "When we reflect with gratitude before rest, we return all borrowed energy back to stillness. Every moment, every encounter, even every discomfort, has offered something — a fragment of understanding, a whisper of truth. Reflection transforms those fragments into light."

He paused, his hands folded loosely in his lap. "Let me tell you a story," he said softly.

The Lantern Maker's Evening

In a quiet town nestled by the hills lived a lantern maker named Ravi. Every day, he crafted delicate lamps of coloured glass and clay, shaping them with care and devotion. His hands bore the marks of his work — burns from the kiln, scars from broken glass

— yet each evening, when he lit his final lantern, his eyes shone with peace.

One night, his apprentice asked him, "Master, why do you always sit in silence before you leave the workshop? The day's work is done — why not go home and rest?"

Ravi smiled. "Because the day's work is only complete when the heart remembers," he said.

He gestured toward the rows of glowing lanterns. "Each of these lights carries a story — one may have cracked, another may have turned out more beautiful than I imagined. Some sold quickly, some were ignored. But before I close my eyes, I give thanks for them all — for they are all part of my journey. Gratitude gathers what is scattered."

The apprentice watched as the old man knelt, lighting one last lantern. "This," Ravi said, "is for all I did not see — for the unseen blessings, the lessons hidden in mistakes, the invisible hands that guided me. When I light this, I remember that even in the dark, there is grace."

Years later, when Ravi passed on, the townspeople found a letter near his bench. It read: *"Each day ends not when the sun sets, but when the heart gives thanks. Only then can rest become renewal."*

Guruji let the silence after the story linger — a silence rich with meaning, as if the whole hall was breathing in the lantern's glow.

He then said gently, "Like the lantern maker, we too must end our day with light. To close the day without reflection is to leave the flame unattended. But when we pause — just for a few minutes — and recall what we received, what we learned, and who we shared it with, we transform experience into wisdom."

He leaned forward slightly, his voice soft yet resonant. "Gratitude at night is not just memory — it is alignment. It gathers the mind that has wandered through the day, and brings it home. It tells the soul, 'All is well, and all has meaning.'"

A hush fell over the devotees. The night breeze moved through the trees, carrying the scent of earth after dew.

Guruji continued, "The one who closes each day with awareness," he said, "awakens lighter, freer, and closer to the divine rhythm of life. Gratitude at dusk is not an ending — it is the gentle turning of the soul toward light."

Kiran asked, "Guruji, which moments from today are worth pausing to acknowledge before sleep, and what quiet lessons did they leave behind?"

Kiran's question hung in the air — tender, searching, almost prayer-like.

Guruji looked around, his gaze sweeping over each face illuminated by the flickering lamp. "Kiran," he began, his voice gentle yet deep, "every day is a scripture written by the Divine. But few pause long enough to read it before the night turns the page."

He continued, "We often think gratitude must rise only for the grand gestures — success, love, praise, or kindness given. But the true moments worthy of acknowledgement are the quiet ones — the pauses between action and reaction, the breath between anger and understanding, the instant where one chooses patience over pride. These are not loud victories, yet they hold the fragrance of spiritual maturity."

Then, after a long silence, Guruji shared a story.

"There was once a humble fisherman named Devraj who lived by a vast lake. Each evening, after returning with his modest catch, he would sit by the water's edge, watching the ripples fade under the sunset. One day, his son asked, 'Father, why do you sit here so long? The work is done.' Devraj smiled and replied, 'I wait for the lake to settle. Only when the ripples calm do I see the reflection of the sky clearly. The day is no different, my son. I let my heart settle so I can see which parts of the day were blessings in disguise and which were lessons dressed as mistakes.'"

Guruji paused, letting the words find their home in everyone's heart.

"Reflection before sleep," he said, "is like sitting by that lake. We allow the disturbances of the day to settle, and in that stillness, the truth of each moment reveals itself. Perhaps you spoke kindly when you could have been harsh — that's a victory of the heart. Perhaps someone's criticism hurt you — yet it showed you your hidden sensitivity, a mirror for self-knowledge. Or maybe you simply noticed the colour of the evening sky and felt peace for no reason — that too is divine grace whispering, 'I am here.'"

He leaned back slightly, eyes half-closed. "The moments worth acknowledging are not those that made you *appear* great, but those that made you *feel* whole. Gratitude, then, becomes the evening lamp — not lit to chase darkness, but to remember that the light never left."

Guruji then softly added, "So before sleep, pause and ask — which ripples in my lake still move tonight? And then, breathe… until your heart becomes a mirror of still waters. That is how one ends the day in the embrace of gratitude."

Guruji gazed at the circle of devotees, the golden glow of the *jyoti* flickering upon his serene face. The night had deepened; the fragrance of sandalwood lingered softly in the air, mingling with the silence that only true reflection brings. After their long evening of introspection, Guruji's voice rose again — gentle, steady, and resonant like the final note of a raga.

He said, "Let me narrate a story."

The Gratitude Jar

The devotees straightened slightly, their eyes attentive.

"There was once a young woman named Jasmine," Guruji began, "whose heart carried a constant restlessness. Her eyes always searched for what was missing — a better job, more love, a sense of purpose that forever seemed just out of reach. Even in moments of joy, her mind whispered, *'It's not enough.'*"

"One evening, after a particularly difficult day, she sat alone in her small room, feeling the weight of dissatisfaction press upon her chest. Her grandmother's old words echoed in her mind: *'When you cannot see the blessings around you, begin to count them — one by one.'*"

"Jasmine hesitated, but something within her stirred — a faint longing to see life differently. She found an old glass jar from the kitchen, tore a small piece of paper, and wrote, 'Today I am grateful for the sound of rain on my window.' It felt insignificant… yet peaceful. The next night, she wrote again: 'Grateful for my mother's voice on the phone.' And the next night, another — 'For the stranger who smiled when I was lost in thought.'"

Guruji paused, his tone softening, "Days turned to weeks, and weeks to months. Some nights, her gratitude flowed easily, like a stream finding its rhythm. Other nights, she wrote with tears — *'Grateful for the lesson of being ignored,'* or *'Grateful for pain that taught me patience.'* Slowly, her perception began to shift. What she once called ordinary began to shimmer with quiet significance."

He looked around the hall. "One day, a year later, Jasmine decided to open her jar. She sat by her window and unfolded each note, one by one. Some were faded, others smudged with fingerprints and tears. But as she read them aloud, she realised something profound — her life had not been empty at all. The blessings had always been there, like stars hidden behind clouds. Gratitude had simply cleared her sky."

A tender smile crossed Guruji's lips as he said, "In that moment, Jasmine understood that gratitude was never about what she *had*, but about how she *saw*. It was the lens that revealed life's sacred texture. Even the smallest grace — a sip of warm tea, a kind word, a quiet breath — became an offering to the Divine."

He paused and then said softly, "Now she carries not a jar, but a heart — a living vessel of remembrance. Each day, she drops her awareness like a note inside it. That invisible jar fills endlessly, not with possessions, but with presence."

Guruji closed his eyes briefly, as though listening to the silence that followed.

"My dear ones," he said finally, his tone a whisper of compassion, "each of us carries such a jar within — unseen but eternal. Every act of recognition, every breath of thankfulness, every humble acknowledgement of grace fills it quietly. And when life feels empty, it is not because blessings are missing — it is because we have forgotten to look."

He opened his palms toward the lamp and said, "May your nights become a ritual of remembrance — a silent filling of your inner jar. For gratitude does not add to life; it reveals that life itself has always been enough."

The devotees sat still — hearts illumined, eyes moist, the night now fragrant not just with sandalwood but with understanding.

Somewhere outside, a gentle breeze moved through the trees, as if the universe itself had bowed in quiet agreement.

The Buddha Hall lay quiet now, emptied of its human congregation, yet it still breathed with the warmth of presence, as if the very walls had absorbed the resonance of the day's devotion. The night sky stretched wide and infinite, dusted with silver starlight that shimmered faintly over the courtyard. A gentle wind stirred the leaves, carrying with it the soft scent of jasmine and the distant echo of the day's laughter. Frogs croaked their nocturnal hymns, insects hummed a rhythmic undertone, and the world itself seemed attuned to a subtle, invisible music—a quiet reminder that the night, too, is a teacher.

Akshaya, Padma, Vasudeva, Kiran, Vidyarthi, Aastha, and Abhirami, having finished their meals, gathered around the fireplace. The flames leapt gently into the cool night air, shadows dancing across their faces, as warmth and friendship spread together in waves. Conversation meandered naturally: reflections on the day's teachings, laughter at small missteps, reverent discussion of Guruji's insights, and contemplations on the subtle threads connecting each story and lesson.

Soon, the circle widened. Kiran, Sam, Alice, Sofia, Bhavya, Aarna, Dev, and John joined, cheeks glowing from a brief evening stroll, their laughter weaving seamlessly with the crackle of firewood. Nita, Lalitha, Rohith, and Sujitha arrived next, adding warmth, both physical and emotional, to the gathering. Moments later, Abhilasha, Akanksh, Akshatha, Apeksha, and Roopa appeared, their expressions alive with quiet reflection, carrying the weight and wonder of the day's learning. Behind them, Kieron, Astyn, Espen, Greta, and Divyani joined, bringing the subtle hum of curiosity and presence that only shared awareness can generate. Each arrival completed the circle, a living mandala of seekers, connected through attention, heart, and shared intention.

A hush fell as Vidyarthi's calm, expectant voice rose above the murmurs. "Time for Apeksha's story…"

All eyes turned toward her. Apeksha inhaled deeply and narrated the story.

The Lantern Maker and the Petal

A long time ago, in a quiet village by the river, there lived a lantern maker named Rohan. Each evening, he would light the lanterns he had crafted and place them along the riverbank. The glow would ripple across the water, guiding travellers and fishermen safely home. Though his work was humble, Rohan took immense care, polishing each lantern until it shone like captured sunlight.

One evening, as he walked along the river, he noticed a single lotus petal floating atop the water. It drifted slowly, carried by currents and wind alike, fragile yet unyielding. Rohan bent down to pick it up, marvelling at its delicate beauty. The petal reminded him that even the smallest things could carry brilliance — unseen by many, yet radiant in their own way.

The next day, he began to integrate this lesson into his craft. He paid closer attention to the curves of each lantern, the subtle interplay of light and shadow, the way the flame danced in the glass. The villagers began to notice the change — the lanterns glowed with a warmth that felt like more than mere illumination; it was as if they carried a whisper of the river, the sky, and the quiet patience of the lotus petal.

Months later, a great storm swept through the village. Trees bent, roofs were torn, and the river swelled. The villagers feared the loss of Rohan's lanterns. But when the storm passed, they saw that each lantern had survived, standing quietly, casting its soft light across the wet earth. The villagers realised something profound: it was not only the craftsmanship that preserved them, but the care, attention, and reverence Rohan had poured into his work — the gratitude he felt for each material, each moment, and each life he touched through his lanterns.

Rohan smiled as he retrieved a small lotus petal that had landed beside his workbench, and whispered to himself, "Even the smallest gift, acknowledged and nurtured, can light the world in ways we cannot predict."

From that day onward, the villagers learned to see the beauty in the overlooked — a child's laughter, a kind word, the quiet hum of the river at dawn. And slowly, they too began to live with a heart open to gratitude, discovering that the light of care and attention, once kindled, could never be extinguished.

As her story drew to a close, Padma whispered softly, almost to herself but just audible enough to touch the circle, "It's time to rest… tomorrow awaits with its own lessons."

One by one, the devotees rose. Movements were gentle and mindful, attuned to the sacred quiet of the night. The world outside, cloaked in darkness, seemed to cradle them tenderly.

PART TWO

Deepening and Mastery of Gratitude

The Alchemy of Gratitude

"Ingratitude is not the absence of blessings, but blindness to them. The shadows we fear are only places where our awareness has yet to shine."

\- *Shree Shambav*

CHAPTER IV

Shadows of Ingratitude

"Every thought is a note, every emotion a vibration. Gratitude is the harmony that tunes the soul to the rhythm of creation."

– Shree Shambav.

Synopsis

The chapter illuminates the unseen landscapes of the heart where gratitude often struggles to bloom. Beneath our longing for peace and fulfilment lie hidden resistances — fear of loss, unhealed wounds, unmet expectations, and the subtle conditioning of scarcity that convinces us we are never enough. These inner shadows distort perception, drawing our attention to what is missing rather than what is present.

Through reflective insights, stories, and meditative contemplation, this chapter invites the reader to see ingratitude not as a flaw, but as a teacher — a mirror revealing where love, acceptance, and understanding have yet to reach. By gently observing our complaints, comparisons, and emotional patterns, we uncover the deeper truths they conceal: unacknowledged pain, forgotten tenderness, and the soul's longing for connection.

When we meet these shadows with compassion, they begin to dissolve, revealing the quiet strength of the heart. Gratitude then ceases to be an effort; it becomes a natural state of being — a return to innocence, clarity, and wholeness. The journey through ingratitude, paradoxically, becomes the doorway to our most authentic appreciation of life.

Morning in Kanchipuram unfolded in a serene embrace — the kind that touches both air and soul. The wind carried a gentle coolness, whispering through the leaves like an unseen hymn. Tree branches swayed in graceful rhythm, and flowers nodded softly, their petals glistening with the last pearls of rain. The earth, still damp from the night's tender showers, exhaled the scent of renewal — that sacred fragrance only dawn after rain can offer.

Within this quiet harmony, the **Buddha Hall** stood poised in silence, its atmosphere rich with anticipation. Devotees had gathered long before sunrise, their hearts steady, eyes softened by reverence. A stillness deeper than sound filled the space — that living silence born not of emptiness, but of presence. Each breath felt like a prayer awaiting completion.

Then, faintly at first, they heard it — **the soft, measured footsteps of Guruji** approaching. It was as though the sound itself bowed before entering the hall. The murmuring breeze seemed to still, and the very air deepened with awareness. When Guruji appeared, his gentle smile carried the warmth of countless dawns, dissolving the last traces of fatigue and thought.

With palms joined in **Atma Namaste**, he greeted each soul not as followers, but as reflections of the same divine essence. His eyes, calm yet radiant, seemed to look beyond faces — seeing directly into hearts. Slowly, with the grace of one who moves in rhythm with eternity, Guruji walked to his **asana** and seated himself.

A brief pause followed — timeless in its quietness. The hall, the trees, even the distant rustle of leaves seemed to bow into stillness. In that pause, the world itself appeared to inhale peace. And as Guruji closed his eyes for a moment, a subtle shift filled the space — an almost imperceptible pulse of serenity spreading through all who sat before him.

The morning no longer belonged to Kanchipuram alone. It belonged to that sacred silence shared between teacher and disciples — where words had yet to begin, but truth had already arrived.

The Roots of Resistance

"Many," Guruji began softly, "struggle to feel grateful—not because they are unkind or unaware, but because their hearts are tired. Gratitude is not difficult because life lacks blessings; it feels difficult because pain still echoes within."

He closed his eyes briefly, as if listening to something far beyond words. "Imagine a tree that has faced many storms. Its branches twist toward the light, but its roots… some roots grow around stones. Some roots were broken once and healed crooked. Yet, it still stands. Likewise, the human heart grows through seasons of joy and loss, love and betrayal, hope and despair. Gratitude struggles to bloom not because it is absent, but because the soil of the heart is sometimes compacted by pain."

He looked up, eyes glistening with compassion. "Neuroscience tells us that the brain, when repeatedly exposed to stress, begins to favour caution over openness, fear over wonder. It is not our fault—it is the body's way of saying, 'I have been hurt before.' Trauma builds neural pathways that look for danger even in safety. Thus, when gratitude asks us to soften, the mind hesitates; it wonders, *'What if I am hurt again?'*"

A hush fell over the devotees. The sound of the night wind moved through the open windows like a sigh of remembrance.

Guruji continued, his tone deepening into tenderness. "The shadows of ingratitude are not signs of moral weakness; they are echoes of unhealed pain. When someone cannot feel thankful, it is not because they lack goodness—it is because their soul is asking for gentleness. Every complaint hides a wound; every resistance is a shield. Gratitude begins not by forcing appreciation, but by sitting beside these unhealed places and saying, 'I see you. You are safe now.'"

He rose from his seat, walking slowly toward the open veranda, where the moonlight pooled like liquid silver. "Think of a river obstructed by stones. The water does not curse the rocks; it flows around them, over time polishing even the roughest edges. The same is true of healing. Gratitude flows naturally once we stop fighting our pain and begin listening to it. It is the whisper that follows acceptance—the soft, almost imperceptible reminder that life, despite everything, is still offering itself to us."

He turned back toward the devotees and smiled. "So, when you cannot feel grateful, do not shame yourself. Instead, trace the root of that resistance. Beneath it, you will always find a story—a moment where love was lost, trust was broken, or hope was wounded. Sit with that moment, not as a judge, but as a healer. Gratitude will return not as an effort, but as a reunion."

He sat again, folding his hands gently. "Gratitude is not the denial of pain—it is the transformation of pain into wisdom. And that wisdom always begins with tenderness toward oneself."

The silence that followed was heavy yet comforting, like rain settling into dry soil.

Why Gratitude Feels Hard

Rohith asked, "Guruji, where in our lives does gratitude struggle to take root, and what memories or wounds might be nurturing that resistance?"

The hall fell into stillness once again after Rohith's question. His tone was gentle but weighted with sincerity—the kind that comes not from curiosity but from lived experience. The soft glow of oil lamps shimmered across faces that had grown reflective, perhaps remembering their own invisible knots—the places within where gratitude seemed to fade into silence.

Guruji looked at Rohith for a long moment, his gaze steady, compassionate. "Your question," he said softly, "is like holding up a mirror to the human heart."

He leaned slightly forward, his voice deep and rhythmic, like a calm current moving through still waters.

"Gratitude struggles to take root in the same places where love once went unheard, where pain was denied, where expectation turned into disappointment. It hesitates in the soil of memory that was never given sunlight to heal. These are the unseen gardens within us—some fertile, some fallow, some buried beneath stones of old hurt."

He paused, then continued, his tone more intimate now.

"Every heart carries its own terrain. In one, there may be the barren field of *betrayal*—trust once planted there was never watered again. In another, the frozen valley of *unworthiness*—where one was told, directly or silently, 'you are not enough.' And in yet another, the dense forest of *loss*—where love once grew abundantly but was cut down too soon. Gratitude struggles not because it cannot grow, but because it is afraid to grow where the sun of tenderness has not yet reached."

The devotees sat in rapt attention. Outside, a faint breeze entered through the window, stirring the flame of the lamp.

Guruji's eyes softened as he spoke further. "Imagine planting a seed in soil hardened by years of drought. You cannot force it to bloom on demand. You must first soften the ground—pour water gently, remove the thorns, and let light touch it again. The same is true of our hearts. Gratitude will not root in hardened emotion. It requires tenderness, patience, and the courage to revisit what we've tried to forget."

He looked around the hall slowly, his words carrying a quiet radiance.

"Often, we try to practice gratitude as a discipline—writing lists, repeating affirmations—but inside, the heart whispers, *'You've not heard my pain.'* The practice becomes hollow when it does not meet the wound. Real gratitude doesn't begin with saying, *'I am thankful for everything.'* It begins when you can say, *'I understand why it has been hard to be thankful.'* That is where healing begins."

A long silence followed, then Guruji said softly, "Let me tell you a story."

The Lantern Maker

In a small town by the river, there lived a lantern maker named Rayan. Each evening, he crafted lamps for the temple festival—delicate paper shades that glowed like captured moons. But one year, tragedy struck. His young apprentice, who had been like a son to him, drowned when the river flooded.

From that day, Rayan stopped making lanterns. The tools gathered dust, the oil dried up, and his home grew dim. People came to console him, but their words only echoed his emptiness.

Seasons passed. One night, during the festival of lights, Rayan wandered to the riverbank. The town shimmered with lanterns floating gently downstream—hundreds of them. Their reflections danced on the water like scattered stars. He stood there for a long time, heart heavy yet stirred by something unnamed.

Then, from behind him, a small voice said, "Master, didn't you teach me that every flame carries a prayer?" It was the voice of his late apprentice—alive in memory, tender and real. In that instant, Rayan realised the river had not taken his light away—it had only changed its form.

He returned home, lit his lamp, and began to craft again—not out of obligation, but out of remembrance. Each lantern he made carried a silent prayer, each flame a whisper of love transformed.

And as he sent the first lantern down the river, he murmured, "I thank you for teaching me that love never ends—it only changes its place in the world."

Guruji looked up after a pause, his voice soft as the dying embers of a lamp.

"Gratitude struggles to take root in the soil of grief, yet that is also where it finds its greatest depth. When we face our wounds with awareness and compassion, they cease to be barriers—they become the very ground from which gratitude blossoms."

He looked toward Rohith and added gently, "So, when you feel resistance, don't fight it. Sit with it, as Rayan did by the river. Listen to what it has to say. For behind every resistance is remembrance, and behind every remembrance—if met with love—waits rebirth."

The silence that followed was not empty—it was sacred.

Scarcity vs. Abundance

Guruji sat quietly for a long moment before speaking. The hall was still, yet filled with an invisible tension — the kind that exists between who we think we are and what life is trying to show us. The lamp beside him flickered softly, and his eyes, deep as a silent ocean, reflected its golden flame.

He said slowly, "Scarcity and abundance are not outer realities. They are inner lenses through which you look at the same world."

The words seemed simple, yet they carried a gravity that sank deep into everyone's heart.

Guruji continued, "When the mind operates from scarcity, it lives in comparison — constantly measuring what it lacks. It counts the blessings of others but forgets its own. This scarcity is not poverty of possessions, but poverty of perception. It filters life through absence — through what is not — and therefore, it cannot see what already *is*."

A gentle wind passed through the open doors, and Guruji pointed to it, saying, "You see the breeze touch the leaves, yet you do not see the breeze itself. Scarcity works the same way — invisible, but its effects ripple through your life. You may have love, but you'll feel unloved. You may have an opportunity, but you'll feel limited. You may have enough, yet you'll whisper, 'It's not enough.'"

He paused, and his tone softened. "Gratitude is not born from having everything. It's born from *seeing* what is already given. Even a single drop, when seen with awareness, reflects the entire ocean of life."

He looked toward the devotees and said, "Imagine a man standing at a well. The well is full, but he lowers his bucket half-heartedly, afraid there may not be enough water. He pulls it back too soon, only to find it empty. Scarcity made him withdraw before life could fill him. But another man lowers his bucket with trust — and waits. His faith allows him to draw abundance, not because the well changed, but because his *lens* did."

A silence fell. You could hear the faint sound of a bell from the distant temple.

Guruji continued, “Scarcity narrows your sight — it whispers fear. Abundance expands it — it sings gratitude. To live abundantly is not to possess more, but to perceive more. To recognise even the smallest blessing as sacred — that is abundance.”

He then smiled gently and concluded, “Shift your gaze, and the world shifts with you. Scarcity says, ‘I’ll be grateful when I have enough.’ But gratitude says, ‘I have enough — therefore, I am grateful.’ The difference is not in what you hold, but in *how you see.* Shifting perception from deficiency to sufficiency is the first step in dissolving all resistance.”

The hall remained in silence. Yet in that silence, something profound had moved — as if each heart had suddenly realised that the infinite was already within reach, hidden behind the fog of its own limited gaze.

The Lens That Limits You

Sujitha asked, “Guruji, in which areas of our life do we still operate from a sense of scarcity, and how can we begin to recognise and honour what is already enough?”

Guruji turned his gaze toward Sujitha, who sat with her palms resting softly on her knees, her eyes earnest yet heavy with an unspoken question.

He smiled, that kind of smile which carried both compassion and quiet knowing, and said, "Sujitha, the sense of scarcity hides in places we least expect. It wears many masks — fear, comparison, guilt, even ambition. It doesn't always shout; sometimes it whispers. It whispers in the thought, *'I am not enough,' 'I don't have enough,'* or *'I must do more to deserve happiness.'*"

He paused, letting the silence breathe between his words.

"Scarcity is like a fog that covers the garden of your life. The flowers are there — blooming — but you only see the mist. You chase more light, more water, more seeds, not realising that the fog itself is what blinds you from the abundance already present."

The devotees listened intently. Some nodded slowly; others lowered their gaze in contemplation.

Guruji continued, "Scarcity seeps into our relationships. When we feel unworthy of love, we begin to bargain for it — giving to be appreciated, speaking to be heard, helping to be seen. Gratitude cannot bloom in such soil, for it grows only in unconditional presence. When you recognise that love already exists in you and flows through you, you stop demanding and start appreciating. That's when connection becomes sacred."

He looked toward the back of the hall, where the breeze carried the faint sound of a bird.

"In our work too, scarcity hides," he said. "We often strive not from creativity, but from fear — fear of being irrelevant, unseen, or left behind. When action arises from scarcity, it drains you. But when it springs from gratitude — from the recognition that life has already given you a place to serve — your work becomes prayer. Every effort, then, is an offering, not a transaction."

He reached for a flower petal that had fallen near his mat and held it up.

"Look at this petal. It does not compare itself with the whole flower. It simply fulfils its role in the fragrance of the bloom. Each petal completes the flower, just as each moment completes life. But we often live as if something is missing — like a petal trying to be the whole blossom. Gratitude allows you to see completion, even within incompleteness."

His tone softened even more, and his voice seemed to dissolve into the stillness of the hall.

"Sujitha, abundance is not what you gather. It's what you *see* and *feel.* To begin recognising it, slow down. Pause in your daily rhythm. Ask yourself — *what is already here? What am I overlooking because I'm too busy seeking?* You'll realise that the warmth of sunlight, the rhythm of your breath, the presence of those who love you — all are quiet forms of abundance waiting to be honoured."

He then closed his eyes briefly and said, "When you stop counting what's missing, you begin to multiply what's present. Scarcity divides the heart; gratitude unites it. The shift begins not in having more, but in seeing more. Once you learn to see through the lens of sufficiency, every small moment becomes sacred — every breath, a reminder that you already have enough to live fully, love deeply, and give freely."

Emotional Shadows

Guruji let the words land like a stone dropped into still water, and the circle felt the ripples.

There is a subtle logic to why gratitude sometimes feels impossible: our hearts carry rooms we have not entered. In those rooms live old feelings — envy, guilt, resentment, shame, fear — that act like curtains across the windows. From the outside, the home looks whole, but from the inside, the light is dim. Gratitude asks us to open the curtains; emotional shadows ask us to stay small, protected, and suspicious of warmth.

What these shadows do

- **They narrow attention.** Fear trains the mind to scan for danger; envy makes us count what others have; guilt keeps us replaying faults. The nervous system becomes biased toward threat, and so the brain filters out the small, safe, nourishing things that invite gratitude.

- **They stiffen the heart.** Unresolved resentment tightens the chest. Guilt tightens the jaw. Energetically, the heart field constricts and cannot receive the subtle currency of appreciation.

- **They make gratitude feel foreign.** When your inner story is "I'm not good enough" or "I was harmed," a sincere "thank you" can feel dishonest — like wearing someone else's clothes.

The House with Many Doors

Imagine your heart as a house. Some doors open onto gardens of light; others lead to cellars where old losses and unspoken words are boxed. If you keep the cellar locked and never sweep it, mould grows and smells seep upward, affecting the whole house. Gratitude is like opening the windows and letting sun and air move through; to let that happen, you must visit the cellars, name the mould, and clear it gently — not to live there, but to reclaim the whole home.

The Blacksmith and the Rusted Blade

There was once a blacksmith, Arjun, who forged the finest blades in his valley. One winter he found he could not temper steel properly — each sword cracked under the hammer. Frustrated, he blamed the metal and cursed the cold. A travelling elder watched him work and asked, "When did you last clean your forge?" Arjun scoffed — his tools had been used for years. The elder simply said, "A rusty tool spoils the art."

So Arjun scrubbed his anvil, heated and freed the rust from the tongs, and mended a cracked bellows. As he cleaned, he found a small, old nail embedded in the anvil's crevice — a remnant of some past repair. Removing it changed the balance of his work; the metal began to sing under his hammer again. He realised the fault had not been in the steel but in neglect — neglected tools, neglected care, neglected shadows.

Like Arjun, when we clear the small, stubborn blocks inside us — the old guilt, the hidden anger, the shame tucked away — our capacity to temper life with gratitude returns. The craft of living works again.

Practical, tender steps to meet and release your shadows

- **Name it (2–5 minutes).** Sit with a notebook. Write one emotion that repeatedly blocks you (fear, envy, guilt, resentment). Write where you feel it in the body and when it most often appears. Naming reduces its charge.

- **Witness without fixing (3–7 minutes).** Breathe into the sensation for five slow breaths. Say silently: "I notice fear is here." Don't explain, argue, or solve—simply witness. Witnessing creates safety.

- **Ask gentle questions (compassionate inquiry).** Where did this feeling first appear? What did it try to protect me from? Listen like you would to a frightened child. This locates the root so it can be healed.

- **Small ritual of release (simple & symbolic).** Write one line to the feeling — e.g., "I see you, fear. Thank you for protecting me. I release you now." Tear or burn the paper safely, or put it into water. Ritual moves the heart beyond thought.

- **Re-pattern with gratitude micro-practices.** After the release, name one small thing you can appreciate — breath, a cup of tea, a steady hand. Repeat the breath/notice cycle. This begins to build new neural grooves of openness.

- **Boundaries & repair.** If resentment is sustained by a relationship, pair inner work with an outer step: set one clear boundary, or choose a small reconciliatory gesture if safe. Healing is both inward and relational.

- **Get help when needed.** If trauma or shame is profound, seek a compassionate therapist or trusted guide. Tender, professional holding dissolves shadows more kindly and safely than pushing alone.

Why does this lead to authentic gratitude?

Meeting your shadows is not about denying pain or forcing cheerfulness. It's about clearing the blockages that make gratitude seem like an act of betrayal to your suffering. When the old hurts are acknowledged and felt, they lose the power to confuse the present. Then gratitude can arise spontaneously — not as a forced smile but as a fuller bandwidth: you can hold ache and appreciation together.

A short guided micro-practice you can do (3 minutes)

- Sit quietly and breathe three slow full breaths.

- Bring to mind one persistent negative feeling. Place a hand where you feel it.
- Silently say: "I notice you. I am with you." Breathe into that spot three times.
- Name one small, undeniable gift in this moment (a breath, a roof, a friend). Allow both the feeling and the gift to coexist. End with a slow exhale.

Shadows are not moral failures; they are invitations. They point to a place that wants tenderness and healing. When you meet them — with curiosity, boundaries, ritual, and sometimes help — gratitude stops being a brittle practice and becomes the natural glow of a healed hearth.

Fear, Guilt, and the Hidden Blocks

Akshaya asked, "Guruji, which recurring emotion most clouds our ability to appreciate life fully—and how might we meet it with compassion instead of resistance?"

For a few moments, Guruji said nothing. The silence itself became a teacher — a mirror in which everyone began to see their own reflection.

Then, slowly, Guruji spoke — his tone neither analytical nor abstract, but deeply human, as though he were touching the pulse of life itself.

Guruji said, "The emotion that most clouds our ability to appreciate life is *fear*.

Not just fear of failure or rejection, but the subtler fears — fear of loss, fear of change, fear of not being enough, fear of being forgotten. These quiet tremors beneath the surface of the mind distort perception. They make the heart cautious, the senses dim, and the present moment appear fragile rather than full."

He looked toward Akshaya and continued, "When fear lingers too long, it begins to weave stories. It tells you that love must be earned, that joy is temporary, and that gratitude is naïve. Slowly, you start protecting yourself from the very things meant to heal you."

The Mirror and the Mist

Guruji's gaze softened.

"Imagine a mirror in a quiet room," he said. "The mirror does not create beauty; it merely reflects it. But when mist gathers on its surface, the reflection blurs. The world outside hasn't changed — the mist only hides what is.

Fear is that mist. It clouds the mirror of awareness, blurring our ability to see the blessings that surround us. The purpose of spiritual practice, then, is not to polish life — but to clear the mist."

He paused, letting the analogy sink in.

"Compassion," he continued, "is the warmth that dissolves that mist. You cannot fight mist with aggression; you can only invite the sun. Likewise, you cannot fight fear by force; you meet it with gentleness — by seeing its roots and holding it tenderly."

The Weaver and the Thread of Fear

"There once lived a weaver named Amara," Guruji began. "She crafted exquisite fabrics admired by the whole village. But one day, her loom broke during a festival order. Afraid of disappointing her patrons, she began weaving hurriedly on a damaged frame. The fabric lost its grace. Threads tangled, patterns collapsed, and what once was art became chaos.

Weeks passed, and her fear of failing deepened. She avoided the loom altogether. One morning, an old traveller came to her shop. Seeing the dust on her tools, he asked, 'Why have you abandoned your gift?'

Amara sighed, 'Because I cannot weave beauty anymore. My threads always tangle.'

The traveller smiled gently and said, 'Then your task is not to weave — it is to untangle.'

He helped her sit again before the loom. Together they removed the knots, one by one — slowly, patiently, without judgment. As she untangled the threads, tears rolled down her cheeks. With each knot undone, she realised the knots were never in the loom — they were in her heart. The fear of imperfection had bound her creativity. By meeting her fear with compassion instead of avoidance, her art returned to life — richer, freer, more luminous."

Guruji looked up. "So it is with us. Life's threads tangle when fear goes unseen. But when met with patience, fear transforms into clarity. Compassion doesn't erase fear — it gives it a language, a place to rest."

How Fear Contracts Gratitude

"Fear," Guruji said softly, "contracts awareness. When the nervous system is in survival mode, it can only perceive threat, not abundance. The body tenses, the breath shortens, and gratitude — which requires openness — cannot enter. You cannot drink water while holding your breath.

Likewise, you cannot receive grace while holding tight to fear."

He continued, "Most of our fears come not from the present but from the past — echoes of moments when love was withheld, or pain was unprocessed. The mind carries those echoes like unfinished prayers. Compassion is the act of listening to those prayers — not silencing them, but saying: *I hear you, and I choose peace anyway.*"

Practical Reflection — Meeting Fear with Compassion

- **Pause and Acknowledge:** When you sense fear arising, don't rush to overcome it. Whisper, "Fear is here." This naming diffuses resistance and opens space for observation.
- **Locate it in the body:** Fear often hides as tension — a clenched jaw, a tight chest, a held breath. Breathe into that space; warmth dissolves what willpower cannot.
- **Offer kindness:** Place a hand over that area and say, "You are safe now." These words, when felt sincerely, calm the limbic mind and invite the prefrontal awareness where gratitude lives.
- **Reframe with truth:** Ask, "What is this fear protecting me from?" Often, you will find that

fear seeks safety. Thank it — and then gently lead it toward gratitude: "Despite this fear, I am thankful for what remains steady, present, and kind."

- **Transform through giving:** Nothing loosens fear more than an act of love. Expressing appreciation, even while afraid, rewires the inner pathways. Gratitude becomes not a feeling but a choice that softens the shadows.

The Flame and the Wind

Guruji turned to the flame burning beside him. "See this light? When the wind blows, the flame flickers — but it does not vanish. The flicker does not mean the light is weak; it only means the air is moving. Fear is that wind. Gratitude is the flame. Your work is not to stop the wind, but to protect the flame — to hold it steady, to let it dance without extinguishing."

He smiled softly and said, "When you meet fear with compassion, it becomes humility. When you meet guilt with compassion, it becomes learning. When you meet pain with compassion, it becomes strength. And when you meet all of them with gratitude — life itself becomes prayer."

Awakening Through Awareness

"The first step toward mastery," Guruji said, "is conscious recognition of resistance. Light begins where we look."

The House with Closed Rooms

Imagine your heart as a house. Daylight pours through the windows in the living room—joy, ordinary pleasure, easy gratitude. But other rooms remain shut: the childhood attic with old disappointments, the cellar where shame hides, the storeroom of anxious future scenarios. Until you open the doors and bring a lamp inside, those rooms shape the whole house in the dark. Recognition is simply opening the door and letting a light reveal what's there — not to shame it, but to see it.

The Lighthouse Keeper and the Hidden Lamp

In a coastal town, a lighthouse keeper named Nila tended a great light that guided ships through storms. One moonless night, a storm knocked out several smaller lanterns along the shore. The keeper spent the night searching, finding that some lanterns were full of sand, others had broken wicks, and a few were simply buried under leaves. She did not scold the lanterns; she cleaned them, mended the wicks, and set them back in place.

By morning, the shore glowed again. When a fisher asked how she could restore so many lights in such darkness, Nila answered, "I only looked carefully; the rest was simple care. Darkness cannot hold what attention touches."

The lesson is this: attending, repairing, and re-lighting are ordinary actions that transform a field of shadows into a shoreline of welcome.

Why Recognition Matters

- **It cuts the fog:** Naming a feeling ("This is fear," "This is old guilt") reduces its primitive hold.
- **It opens pathways:** Observing without judgment engages prefrontal awareness and calms the survival circuits.
- **It invites repair:** Once seen, hearts can be tended with concrete care instead of avoidance.
- **It builds momentum:** Small recognitions (and small acts of care) rewire neural pathways toward openness and gratitude.

Practical, Gentle Steps — How to Light the Hidden Corners

- **Observe without editorialising (2–5 minutes).**

  Sit comfortably. Name what's present in one sentence: "I notice tightness in my chest," or "There is anger right now." No, why, no solution—just naming.

- **Map the trigger (5–10 minutes).**

  Ask quietly: When did this come up today? What was said or seen? Note one memory it echoes. Mapping links present sensation to the source.

- **Journal the doorway (5–7 minutes).**

  Write: "Today I noticed ___; I think it connects to ___; one small way I can care for it is ___." Keep entries short. The structure trains attention to land on healing.

- **Gentle witnessing (3 breaths).**

  Place a hand where you feel the emotion. Breathe into that place and say, "I am here with you." This somatic kindness soothes the nervous system.

- **Small repair action (daily micro-step).**

  Do one practical, loving thing for that wound: a conversation, an apology, a boundary, or an offering to yourself (a short walk, a nourishing meal, a 7-minute breath practice). Small repair matters more than grand gestures.

- **Close with gratitude (1 line).**

  End your practice by naming one small, true thing you are grateful for right now. This seals the circuit from noticing openness.

Short Guided Practice — 5 minutes

- Sit. Breathe 3 slow rounds.
- Name one resistance quietly: "I notice ____."
- Place your hand on the area that feels charged. Breathe into it three times.
- Ask: "What story does this want me to hear?" Allow one single image or memory to surface — don't chase it.
- Offer one sentence of kindness: "I see you. You are safe to be felt."
- End: speak one small gratitude aloud. Rest.

Journaling Prompts that Illuminate (use these repeatedly)

- "Tonight I noticed resistance when ____. I think it links to ____. One small kindness I will give this part of me is ____."
- "A shadow I met today taught me ____."
- "One thing I saw clearly today that I had been missing is ____."

Short, structured notes are more powerful than long essays—consistency rewires.

How This Opens the Heart to Authentic Gratitude

Recognition is the bridge. When you stop pushing dark parts away and instead learn to meet them with steady attention and practical care, the heart relaxes. The nervous system downgrades threats and upgrades rewards. Appreciation no longer feels like a forced performance; it arrives naturally, because the house of the heart is whole again—windows open, rooms aired, lanterns mended.

A Small Week Plan (practical & doable)

Day 1 - Name: Use the 5-minute guided practice tonight.

Day 2 - Map: Journal 5 lines: trigger → earliest memory → small care step.

Day 3 - Repair: Do one small repair action (speak, set boundary, self-care).

Day 4 - Witness: Spend 3 minutes breathing into your body's tension.

Day 5 - Gratitude Jar: Drop one written note of thanks into a jar (physical or digital).

Day 6 - Share: Tell one person "thank you" specifically and from the heart.

Day 7 - Reflect: Read your week's notes; notice changes; affirm one intention for the next week.

Be the Lighthouse, Not the Storm

You do not have to banish the storm to guide ships. You only need to tend the light. Recognition, witness, small repair—these are the daily acts that make the inner lighthouse burn steady. Over time, that steadiness turns resistance into a companion and allows gratitude to rise naturally, not as a task, but as the homecoming of the heart.

Lighting the Hidden Corners

Padma asked, "Guruji, what daily practice can help us recognise the first stirrings of ingratitude, allowing us to respond with awareness rather than habit?"

Guruji smiled, his gaze resting softly on the flickering flame of the *Jyoti* before him. Then he turned to Padma and said gently, "Padma, the first stirrings of ingratitude are like the faint tremors that come before an earthquake. Subtle… almost invisible… but they carry the power to shake the foundation of peace if left unnoticed."

He paused, as if to let the silence become a mirror.

"When we feel the first trace of restlessness — a small complaint, a sense that something is missing, or a feeling that life owes us more — that is the whisper of ingratitude. It begins not in grand moments, but in the smallest cracks of attention. The mind forgets what *is*, and begins chasing what *isn't*."

Guruji said, "There was once a gardener who worked in a king's courtyard. Each morning, he would sing as he watered the flowers, grateful for their fragrance and colour. One day, a traveller passed by and asked, 'How can you be so joyful with such simple work?' The gardener smiled, 'Because the flowers bloom for me as much as for the king. Each petal reminds me that life still breathes through me.'

But over time, the gardener's eyes began to wander. He saw the courtiers dressed in silk, the gold ornaments, the grand feasts. Slowly, his song grew softer. His work became duty, not devotion. When the flowers wilted, he blamed the weather. When they bloomed, he barely noticed.

One morning, the king noticed the garden losing its glow and asked him what had changed. The gardener, humbled, said, 'I stopped seeing beauty in what I already had.' The king replied, 'Then, my friend, your eyes grew poor long before the garden did.'"

Guruji looked around the hall. "Ingratitude blinds not the eyes, but the awareness behind them. The way back is through a simple, sacred practice — *Sakshi Smarana* — remembrance through witnessing."

He continued softly, "Each morning, before your mind begins its usual rhythm, pause. Close your eyes and name three blessings that were invisible yesterday. Feel them — not as thoughts, but as warmth in your chest. Maybe it's the breath that returned again. Maybe it's the hand that reached to help you. Maybe it's the silence that gave you rest. This small act shifts the lens through which life is seen. It teaches the heart to notice before it forgets."

Then he added, "And when the day ends, before sleep takes you, replay not your disappointments, but your moments of grace. Gratitude grows not through effort but through remembrance — remembrance of what was already given."

Guruji's voice softened like the dying flame of a lamp.

"The daily practice, Padma, is not to become grateful, but to *remain awake* to the abundance already moving through your life. For every sigh that escapes unnoticed, gratitude waits quietly in the same breath, asking only to be seen."

He looked toward the devotees and said finally, "When awareness becomes your morning prayer and remembrance your evening rest, ingratitude loses its soil. Awareness uproots the habit. Compassion waters the heart. And life, once again, begins to bloom from within."

After a long silence, he opened his eyes, his voice calm yet resonant.

"Before we close this morning's reflection," he said, "let me share with you a story—a story that mirrors the quiet truth we have been touching upon today."

He paused for a breath, his gaze moving across the circle of seekers who awaited his words with the stillness of listening hearts.

The Stone and the Stream

"There was once a young monk," Guruji began softly, "who lived in a tranquil monastery tucked within the folds of the mountains. His days were filled with prayer, discipline, and peace. Yet deep within him, he felt a quiet ache—a sense that something was missing, a subtle resistance to joy.

One morning, he approached his teacher and confessed,
'Master, I have everything I need—food, shelter, knowledge—and yet, I cannot feel grateful. Why does my heart remain unmoved?'

The teacher smiled and said, 'Come, walk with me.'

They walked through the valley where the first light of dawn kissed the dewdrops on the grass. Soon, they reached a stream whose clear waters danced over stones, catching the morning sun in countless shimmering ripples.

The teacher pointed to a large stone resting in the stream.
'Tell me what you see,' he asked.

The monk replied, 'The stone is blocking the water—it cannot flow freely.'

The teacher smiled. 'Look again.'

The monk bent closer. The water wasn't trapped—it was flowing *around* the stone, creating new paths, new sounds, new reflections of light.

The teacher said gently, 'The stone does not stop the stream. The stream adapts, learns, and continues its song. But the stone, too, shapes the water's path. Both serve their purpose.'

The monk frowned. 'So, am I the stone?'

The teacher nodded. 'Yes. Your fears, your resentments, your expectations—they are stones within you. The stream of gratitude is not gone; it simply flows where you allow it. When you stop trying to force the current and instead observe the stones with awareness, life begins to move naturally again.'

Guruji's voice lingered in the air like morning incense. "Years later," he continued, "the monk wrote in his journal:

'The more I tried to feel grateful, the more I resisted life.
When I stopped striving and simply noticed my own resistance, the stones became my teachers, and gratitude flowed around them like water finding its way home.'"

The devotees listened in silence. Outside, the first call of the cuckoo echoed across the fields, blending with the distant rustle of palm leaves.

Guruji looked up and said with deep compassion, "You see, my dear ones, gratitude is not something we chase—it's something we *remember*. It's the natural state beneath all the noise of unmet desires and old wounds. The current of appreciation flows quietly, even when our minds are heavy with thought. What blocks it is not life's imperfection, but our insistence that it must appear a certain way."

He smiled faintly, the kind of smile that carried both grace and knowing.

"When we stop fighting our inner stones—when we learn to see even our pain as part of the path—then gratitude rises like this morning sun: slowly, silently, but inevitably."

He looked at the flame beside him.

"Let gratitude not be an effort of the mind," he said softly,

"but the fragrance of awareness.

When you awaken to what *is*, the current of life begins to sing again."

The devotees bowed their heads. The morning light touched their faces with warmth. Outside, the stream near the garden murmured softly—as if echoing the story itself—flowing, unhurried, around every stone in its way.

After a long pause, Guruji gently spoke, his voice calm and steady, "Let us take the mid-day meal."

A soft hum of anticipation rose among the devotees. Within minutes, they slowly rose from their mats inside Buddha Hall and stepped into the open air. The courtyard was bathed in gentle sunlight, the breeze carrying a mild freshness that hinted at the recent morning rains. As they approached the food center, the air became rich with the aroma of steaming South Indian dishes—the subtle scent of coconut, tempered with the warmth of spices, mingling with the earthy fragrance of the temple grounds.

After their meals, the devotees naturally gravitated toward the shade of the banyan tree. Sam, Alice, Sofia, Bhavya, Aarna, Dev, and John gathered first, their conversation light yet thoughtful, echoing reflections from the morning session. Soon, Akshaya, Padma, Vasudeva, Kiran, Vidyarthi, Aastha, and Abhirami joined them, their presence adding layers of warmth and camaraderie. A few minutes later, Kieron, Astyn, Espen, Greta, and Divyani arrived after a gentle stroll, each carrying a quiet energy of contemplation and engagement.

Nita, Lalitha, Rohith, and Sujitha followed, their faces bright, cheeks flushed from the mild exertion, as if the sun and the breeze themselves had touched their spirits. The circle now felt complete—a living tapestry of seekers, each thread distinct yet interwoven, buzzing with subtle excitement and reflection.

Soon, Abhilasha, Akanksh, Akshatha, Apeksha, and Roopa appeared, carrying cups of herbal tea and coffee. The warmth of the beverages seemed to spread into the very air, mingling with laughter and quiet conversation.

After a comfortable pause, Astyn's voice broke gently into the hum of chatter:

"Apeksha, please… narrate a story."

The Lantern Maker and the Midnight Sky

Apeksha said, "A long time ago, in a quiet village by the edge of a forest, there lived a lantern maker named Ishaan. Every evening, he lit hundreds of small lanterns, filling the village with warm, flickering light. People admired his skill and the beauty of his work, yet few understood the care and intention behind each lantern."

One night, a fierce storm swept through the village. The winds toppled many lanterns, and the villagers despaired. Ishaan, too, felt a pang of frustration. Hours of careful labour had vanished in the blink of an eye. Yet, instead of succumbing to anger, he stepped outside, lanterns in hand, and looked up at the darkened sky. The clouds roiled and shifted, and in the brief moments when the storm paused, he glimpsed the stars peeking through—a quiet reminder that light persists, even when shadows dominate.

Inspired, Ishaan worked silently through the night. For each broken lantern, he crafted a new one, and for each new lantern, he added a small reflection of the moon, a delicate pattern meant to catch even the faintest breeze. By morning, the village was not only restored but illuminated with an unexpected brilliance, more beautiful than before.

The villagers gathered in awe, asking, "Ishaan, how did you find hope in the storm? How did you create such light amid chaos?"

Ishaan smiled gently. "The storm did not take away the light—it only revealed how it must shine," he said. "Gratitude is like the lantern. When we focus only on what is lost, we miss the quiet strength of what remains. Every challenge, every setback, is a chance to notice, to create, to shine more brightly."

From that night on, the villagers remembered his lesson. They began to honour the small acts of care in their lives—the hand that mended a roof, the smile that brightened a morning, the quiet patience of someone standing by without judgment. They realised that gratitude is not only an emotion but a practice—a way of shaping the world like Ishaan shaped his lanterns, one mindful, intentional act at a time.

And so, beneath the vast expanse of sky, the village glowed not just with lanterns, but with hearts awakened to light, aware that even in darkness, grace waits to be noticed and honoured.

Finally, Roopa exhaled softly, a mixture of awe and gentle amusement in her voice.

“It’s time for Guruji’s next session,” she said, breaking the stillness, yet leaving the essence of the story lingering in every heart.

The devotees stirred, some stretching lightly, some sipping the last drops of tea, carrying with them the silent lessons of the tale—ready to return to the hall, minds reflective, hearts open, and spirits gently nourished.

CHAPTER V

Gratitude and the Law of Vibration

"Grace does not erase pain—it transforms it. Through suffering, the soul learns the art of surrender and the courage to love again."

– Shree Shambav.

Synopsis

The chapter delves into the subtle yet powerful energetic dimension of gratitude — revealing it as more than just a pleasant emotion, but as a living vibration that shapes the quality of our reality. Every thought, emotion, and intention emits a frequency, influencing how we experience the world and what we attract into it. Gratitude, in its purest form, resonates with the highest frequencies of love, harmony, and abundance, gently drawing into our lives the reflections of our inner state.

Through simple analogies, reflective practices, and real-life stories, this chapter guides the reader to recognise how energetic alignment works in everyday life. It shows that gratitude is not an outcome of external blessings, but the very force that magnetises them. By consciously choosing appreciation over resistance, one begins to move in rhythm with the universe — synchronising thoughts, emotions, and actions with the flow of grace.

In learning to vibrate with gratitude, we stop chasing fulfilment and start becoming it. Life begins to respond not as a battlefield of desires, but as a harmonious dance of resonance — where every moment, in its own way, whispers, "You are already enough."

The Universe in Motion

Guruji said, "Every atom, every molecule, even the spaces between them, hums with life. From the smallest pebble to the vast oceans, the universe is a symphony of motion—each vibration a note, each rhythm a thread in the fabric of existence. Thoughts, emotions, intentions—they are not separate from this cosmic orchestra. They, too, carry frequency, energy that reaches far beyond the mind, touching the world in subtle, yet profound ways.

Gratitude is a tuning fork. When you feel it genuinely, your frequency rises. The vibration of your heart begins to resonate with the harmony of the universe, aligning you with the flow of abundance, synchronicity, and insight. It is not merely a feeling—it is a signal, a conscious offering to life that whispers: 'I notice. I honour. I participate.'

Imagine a lake at dawn. A single pebble dropped into the still water sends concentric ripples outward, touching every part of the surface. Similarly, a grateful thought, an acknowledgement of beauty or kindness, radiates far beyond your awareness, influencing circumstances, perceptions, and relationships.

Yet, the lake is not passive. If the surface is rough, chaotic, or clouded, the ripples dissipate, distorted. Likewise, negative emotions, fear, or resistance interfere with the pure transmission of gratitude. By cultivating awareness, by observing and consciously choosing appreciation, we smooth the waters of our inner world. Gratitude becomes not just an act—it becomes a state of resonance, a way of being that invites harmony into every interaction.

Thus, to live with awareness of vibration is to participate in the universe consciously. Every thought, every feeling, every act is a note in the grand symphony. When gratitude rises, it tunes your frequency to the music of abundance, allowing life's currents to carry you with ease, clarity, and grace."

The Bellmaker and the Mountain Wind

High in the misty mountains lived a bellmaker named Arun. He spent his days crafting small metal bells, each carefully tuned so that when struck, they would sing with clarity and harmony. Villagers often came to buy his bells, drawn by their purity of sound, though few understood the care and intention woven into each note.

One evening, Arun climbed a ridge to hang his bells along the cliff's edge, allowing the mountain winds to test their resonance. As the wind moved through the valley, the bells chimed, their tones mingling with the rustling leaves and the distant roar of waterfalls. The harmony was mesmerising—a music the valley had never known, though it had existed in the wind and stone all along.

A young traveller passing by stopped, awestruck. "How do you make such a sound?" she asked.

Arun smiled, "The bell itself does not create the music—it only responds. The wind, the air, the stones, everything around it vibrates. Each bell is tuned to notice and participate. Similarly, our thoughts, our gratitude, and our attention are vibrations. When aligned, they harmonise with the universe, creating waves of effect far beyond what we see."

The traveller watched as the wind shifted, carrying some bells into louder resonance and others into gentle whispers. Arun continued, "A heart filled with fear or resistance is like a bell out of tune—the vibration is distorted, the music muffled. Gratitude, even in small measures, raises your resonance. Like these bells in the mountain wind, your frequency touches everything around you, rippling outward in ways unseen but deeply felt."

By the time the traveller descended the ridge, she understood: life is not about forcing harmony—it is about tuning, noticing, and allowing oneself to vibrate in sync with the unseen currents of the world. Every small act of appreciation, every mindful thought, was a note in a symphony of infinite possibility.

And in the valley below, as villagers heard the distant, ethereal chimes echoing through the mountains, many felt an unspoken stirring in their hearts—an invisible invitation to rise in resonance, to notice the harmony already present, and to contribute their own note to the eternal song of life.

Everything Vibrates

Vidyarthi asked, "Guruji, in what ways might the quality of our emotions shape the energy we radiate—whether we are aware of it or not?"

Guruji smiled gently, "Vidyarthi," he began, "our emotions are like the invisible currents of a river. The water may appear calm on the surface, yet beneath, unseen flows carry immense power. Joy, love, gratitude, or peace ripple outward, smoothing stones and nourishing life along the way. Anger, fear, or resentment churn the depths, stirring turbulence that reaches far beyond what we see.

Even when we think our feelings are private, they radiate as subtle vibrations into the world. A smile of genuine warmth can brighten an entire room; a sigh of frustration can quietly weigh down those nearby. Emotions are energy in motion, carrying intention and colour, shaping the perception and experiences of ourselves and others.

Consider a candle in a dark room. Its flame does not ask permission to shine—it illuminates the space around it, revealing beauty, casting shadows, guiding eyes and hearts alike. Our emotions work the same way. Gratitude, compassion, and love act as a clear, steady light, harmonising the environment. Fear, envy, or impatience scatter light, creating distorted reflections and unseen obstacles.

Awareness is the bridge. When we observe our emotional currents without judgment, we recognise the influence we carry. We can choose to nurture feelings that elevate and harmonise rather than those that disrupt and fragment. In this choice lies the art of conscious vibration—the ability to become a beacon, a force that shapes reality not by will alone, but through the subtle power of what we carry within.

Thus, every emotion is a note in the song we offer to the universe. When tuned to clarity, compassion, and gratitude, the song itself becomes a force for connection, healing, and growth. Even a single vibration, when pure, can ripple endlessly, touching lives in ways invisible yet profoundly felt."

The Lantern Maker and the Misty Valley

In a quiet valley shrouded often in mist lived a lantern maker named Liora. Every evening, she would light dozens of lanterns, sending them floating down the river that wound through the village. The villagers said her lanterns were magical—they seemed to carry warmth, hope, and clarity far beyond their gentle glow.

One particularly foggy night, Liora noticed something unusual. A neighbouring lantern maker, in a rush and with a heavy heart, released his lanterns filled with frustration and impatience. They drifted erratically, flickering weakly, some extinguishing before reaching the water's edge. In contrast, Liora's lanterns, lit with calmness and care, floated steadily, illuminating the mist, guiding boats, and reflecting golden light across the riverbanks.

A young apprentice asked her, "Why do your lanterns travel so far and stay lit, while his falter?"

Liora smiled, "Each lantern carries more than fire. It carries the maker's heart. If the hands tremble with anger, or the mind is clouded by fear, the flame struggles. But when intention is gentle, when the heart is aligned with care and gratitude, the light radiates, touching every shadow along the way. Our emotions are like the unseen wind; whether we realise it or not, they shape the journey of every action, every word, every gesture."

From that night onward, the apprentice learned to craft lanterns not just with skill, but with presence—pausing to breathe, to calm the mind, to align the heart. The lanterns became more than tools; they became messengers, carrying hope, warmth, and harmony to every corner of the valley.

Liora whispered to him one evening, "Remember, it is not just the lantern that lights the path. It is the quality of your inner flame that illuminates the world."

And in the valley, as mist rolled through the riverbanks, villagers felt it—an invisible radiance that spoke of care, attention, and the subtle, profound energy of aligned emotions.

Gratitude as an Energetic Signal

The Buddha Hall was hushed in a luminous calm as the afternoon rays softened into a golden haze. The banyan leaves outside shimmered in the breeze, casting dancing shadows across the floor.

After a moment, he looked up and said softly, "Gratitude as an Energetic Signal – *The Frequency of Appreciation.*"

His voice flowed like a slow river—measured, reflective, yet alive with warmth.

"When we feel true gratitude," Guruji continued, "something remarkable happens—not only in the heart but in the very fabric of our energy. The body becomes a transmitter of coherence. Science now mirrors what sages knew long ago—that the heart is not merely a pump, but a field of intelligence, a living instrument of vibration."

He paused, then placed his hand over his heart.

"When you enter a state of appreciation, your heart's electromagnetic field strengthens and synchronises with your brain waves. The two, often in conflict, begin to dance together in rhythm. That inner harmony changes not only your health and mind—it radiates outward. The people near you feel it, the space around you changes, even the air seems lighter."

Aastha listened intently, her brow furrowed slightly in wonder. "Guruji," she asked, "is that why sometimes when someone enters the room, we can feel peace—or tension—even before they speak?"

Guruji smiled gently. "Yes, Aastha. What you call intuition is the heart reading vibration. Every emotion carries a frequency. Anger and fear contract your energy; gratitude expands it. When the heart expands, it becomes a field of communication beyond words—like a silent song the universe can hear."

He leaned back slightly, his tone deepening with story.

"Let me tell you about a farmer who lived by a river. Each morning, he would carry his water pots to the field, humming as he walked. His crops flourished, his cattle were calm, and his home was peaceful. One day, his neighbour asked, 'Why do your plants always bloom brighter than mine? We use the same water, the same soil.'

The farmer smiled and said, 'Because the river listens.'

The neighbour laughed, not understanding.

But the farmer knew—he carried gratitude in his heart each morning, and even the water absorbed it. His fields responded to his vibration."

Guruji's eyes softened as he continued, "Everything in creation is alive, responsive, and listening. The wind, the earth, even the cells in your body—they all respond to your inner music. When gratitude flows through you, it is like tuning an instrument. The body becomes the flute; life, the breath. Together, they create a melody that harmonises with existence."

He paused again, allowing the depth of silence to speak between his words.

"Gratitude is not a polite 'thank you.' It is a *state of coherence.* It tells the universe, 'I am ready. I trust. I see the beauty even in imperfection.' That readiness opens doors you didn't even know existed. Gratitude is the language through which your heart communicates with creation itself."

Kiran raised his hand slowly. "Guruji, what happens when we feel disconnected? When gratitude feels forced?"

Guruji smiled. "Then pause. Don't try to *force* gratitude. Instead, listen—to the pulse of your breath, to the quiet spaces within. You will find that beneath all the noise, gratitude is already there, waiting. It is not something you create; it is something you remember. Just as a radio does not create the signal—it tunes into it."

He lifted a small bell beside him and rang it once. Its tone lingered in the air, long after the sound had faded.

"Do you hear this?" Guruji asked softly. "That vibration travels through space even when your ears no longer catch it. Gratitude works the same way. A single moment of true appreciation continues to ripple through time and space, affecting hearts, events, and unseen realities. You may not perceive it, but the universe does."

Then, in a voice almost like a whisper, he concluded, "When your heart beats in gratitude, it is in conversation with creation. It says, *'I am aligned. I am home.'*"

The devotees sat in silence. The bell's fading echo seemed to merge with their breath, and for a timeless moment, everyone in the hall could *feel* what words could only point toward—that gratitude is not a thought, not a ritual, not even an emotion.

It is a frequency— a living, breathing bridge between the human heart and the pulse of the universe.

The Frequency of Appreciation

Aastha leaned forward slightly. Her eyes carried both curiosity and sincerity as she asked, "Guruji, which moments in our day naturally elevate our energy—and how might we consciously cultivate gratitude to sustain and amplify that vibration?"

Guruji looked at her, his gaze calm yet penetrating. After a pause, he smiled softly. "A beautiful question, Aastha. You see, life offers countless moments where the frequency of gratitude rises naturally, like waves upon the ocean. But we often pass them by—unaware that each is a doorway to higher vibration."

He paused, picking up a flower petal that had fallen from the altar, turning it gently between his fingers. "Imagine this petal," he began. "It receives sunlight, water, and air effortlessly. It does not hoard them, nor fear losing them. It simply participates in the rhythm of life—receiving and giving at once. Gratitude functions the same way. Every time you breathe, see beauty, share kindness, or overcome a challenge, the universe hands you a chance to vibrate in harmony with it."

He placed the petal before him and continued, "There are three sacred thresholds in a day when energy naturally rises.

At *dawn*, when the world awakens, the vibration of possibility is highest. Gratitude for life itself aligns you with creation's first breath.

At *midday*, when light is at its peak, gratitude for clarity and purpose strengthens your will and focus.

And at *sunset*, when the day exhales into stillness, gratitude transforms reflection into peace."

Aastha listened intently, her hands resting gently on her knees. The hall was silent except for the faint crackle of incense. Guruji's words seemed to ripple through the air like unseen currents.

"To sustain that vibration," he continued, "we must learn to *pause* within the current of life. Gratitude cannot bloom in haste—it needs presence. Each moment that naturally elevates energy—whether a child's laughter, the fragrance of rain, or a simple act of kindness—holds a hidden frequency. When you pause and acknowledge it, you amplify that vibration, just as a musician sustains a note to let it fill the space."

He looked toward the open courtyard where sunlight filtered through leaves. "Let me tell you a story," he said, his voice softening like the turning of a page.

The Story of the Potter and the Dawn

In a small village, there lived a potter named Niran. Every morning before sunrise, he would sit before his wheel, listening to the birds stir and the wind whisper through the palms. One day, a traveller stopped by and asked,
"Why do you begin your work so early, before the world has even awakened?"

Niran smiled. "Because the dawn is when the earth's energy is pure. The clay listens better."

The traveller laughed, "Clay listens?"

Niran nodded. "Yes. When I touch it with a grateful heart, it responds. If I rush or worry, it hardens too soon. But when I begin with stillness, each vessel shapes itself effortlessly."

Years later, when the traveller returned, Niran had grown old, but his pots were more beautiful than ever. Their surfaces gleamed with something alive—something that spoke beyond craftsmanship. "You were right," the traveller said softly. "Your clay does listen."

Niran smiled again. "Not just the clay," he said. "Life itself listens to the heart that thanks it."

Guruji turned his gaze back to the devotees. "You see, gratitude is not merely an emotion—it is a tuning fork. When struck with awareness, it aligns every layer of your being with the rhythm of existence. You can awaken that vibration through small acts: watching the morning light, breathing before a meal, or offering thanks before sleep. These are not rituals—they are reminders of the sacred field you live in."

Kiran, sitting beside Aastha, asked gently, "So Guruji, even the smallest moment can become sacred?"

Guruji smiled, eyes gleaming with warmth. "Yes, Kiran. The sacred is not hidden—it breathes through every heartbeat, every shared glance, every act of noticing. When you cultivate gratitude in these ordinary moments, you turn the mundane into music.

Your frequency rises, and life begins to respond to you as a mirror of that vibration."

He paused and added softly, "A grateful heart does not chase miracles—it becomes one."

The hall remained in silence for a long moment. Outside, the banyan leaves shimmered as if nodding in agreement. Aastha lowered her gaze, her eyes moist yet radiant, feeling something shift quietly within her.

And as the devotees sat in that luminous stillness, they realised what Guruji had meant all along—

that gratitude is not something to practice only in prayer,
but a current flowing through every breath,

every smile,

every dawn that breaks and every dusk that closes.

It was life itself, whispering:

"Thank you for noticing."

Resonance and Attraction

"Everything that moves has a tone," Guruji said. "Like tuning forks, our hearts ring at particular frequencies. When those frequencies are held steadily—love, gratitude, generosity—they naturally draw similar notes. When they are held in fear, bitterness, or complaint, they draw those shapes instead. Your inner state is not private; it is a magnet."

Resonance is contagious. Emotions and attitudes are not isolated events inside you; they ripple outward and elicit similar responses. A calm presence soothes a room; a sullen mood tightens it.

Attraction is not magic; it's a match. The world reflects back the energy you carry. If your baseline is appreciation, you notice opportunities, kind people, and synchrony. If your baseline is scarcity, your attention finds lack and confirms it.

You are the filter and the signal. The same circumstance can be felt as a blessing or burden, depending on the frequency with which you bring to mind. Changing the signal (your inner tone) changes the reflection (your outer life).

The Garden and the Songbirds

Imagine a garden where once a week, someone scatters seeds and plays a gentle flute. Birds begin to visit regularly — attracted by both food and song. If the gardener curses the rain and plays a harsh drum, the birds will leave; the garden grows quieter, seed or no seed. The song shapes the atmosphere, and the atmosphere shapes who arrives. Likewise, your inner melody—the quality you sustain—calls people, events, and possibilities to you.

The Perfumer and the Passing Caravan

In a trading town at the edge of a desert lived a perfumer named Salima. Her shop was small, but travellers swore her scents could change a mood. One season, caravans slowed down, and trade dwindled; merchants complained, and the market grew tense with fear. Salima noticed the change, but she did not shrink into worry. Each morning, she mixed one small vial of a new scent—subtle notes of jasmine and sandalwood—then walked to the market and offered a single drop to whoever paused.

At first, people took it politely. But something shifted: the scent softened conversations; a trader apologised for a sharp word; a mother laughed at her child's small joke. Word spread that the perfumer's fragrance seemed to "lift" the market. Caravans began arriving more readily; traders lingered to talk rather than hurry away.

When a sceptical merchant asked how a vial of scent could do so much, Salima replied, "It is not the oil that changes the world. It is the steadiness of an offering—made with gratitude and clarity—that alters the tone of a room. Like attracts like. I offered a little grace, and the market began to remember grace."

How this works inside us

- **Neural habit becomes perceptual habit.** Repeated appreciation trains attention to find corresponding evidence; you begin to *expect* harmony and thus notice it.
- **Energy fields align.** Our bodies and subtle fields respond to steady emotions; people and situations that vibrate similarly feel comfortable and cluster together.
- **Action follows feeling.** When you feel thankful, you act kindly; kind action invites kind response; the loop reinforces itself.

Practical practices — tuning your inner magnet

- **Morning Tone-Setting (2–4 minutes):** On waking, name three small things you genuinely appreciate. Let the feeling swell in the body for three breaths. This sets your baseline.
- **The Micro-Resonance Pause (when triggered):** When irritation or scarcity

appears, stop for one breath, place your hand on your heart, and recall a tiny gratitude (a cup of water, a steady roof). This re-tunes the instrument before it plays.

- **One Intentional Offering (daily):** Give something—praise, help, a moment of listening—without expectation. Your outward offering adjusts the field and invites reciprocity.

- **Evening Resonance Audit (3 minutes):** Before sleep, note two moments where your state drew something you wished for—however small. Record them. Evidence builds trust.

Micro-practice — 60-Second Tuning (use anytime)

- Breathe in deeply.

- Think of one person/place/thing you appreciate now. Let the feeling fill your chest.

- Exhale slowly, imagining that feeling expanding a few feet around you.

- Intend silently: "May this feeling attract what serves the highest good."

- Repeat twice. Then return to your day. The room has changed.

Responsibility and freedom

Guruji's voice softened, "This teaching is not a demand to be happy at every turn. It is an invitation to keep your instrument tuned. You are neither a victim of circumstance nor a solitary island. You are a conductor, and your attention is the baton. When you choose gratitude as the baseline, you become a living magnet for harmony. The world responds in kind—not because you tricked it, but because you matched its truest song."

The hall breathed in that truth. Outside, a breeze moved through the banyan leaves as if a choir had quietly agreed.

Like Attracts Like

Abhirami asked, "Guruji, can you reflect on a recent moment where gratitude shifted our perspective or transformed an outcome? How might consciously practising gratitude in such moments deepen and amplify its effect in the future?"

"Ah — a perfect question," Guruji said, and the hall seemed to lean in. He let a small silence sit like a breath, then spoke as if recalling a living example.

A recent moment — the kitchen's change of heart

"Do you remember today, at the midday meal?" he began. "A small thing happened that changed everything. After we ate, Abhilasha noticed the head cook standing at the edge of the courtyard, wiping her hands, shoulders tense from the morning's labour. No one had thanked her directly; the food was simply there — as if by right. Abhilasha walked over, took the cook's hand, looked her in the eyes, and said slowly, 'We are grateful for your hands today. That sambar held the day together.'"

He paused, smiling at their faces as the memory lit the room. "The cook's face, which had been closed and tired, opened like a flower. She laughed quietly, a small sound of relief. Then she went back to the kitchen and told the staff. By evening, others began to help with small tasks—rinsing pots, folding napkins, bringing water—without being asked. That simple, honest recognition turned labour into service felt and shared. What could have remained invisible became visible; what could have stayed a burden became a relationship."

Why that shift mattered — clarity and feeling?

- **Perception changed immediately.** The kitchen staff moved from feeling unseen to being seen. That transformed posture, tone, and attention.

- **Energy shifted collectively.** A small warmth spread: people loosened, smiled, offered help—sympathy turned into participation.

- **Outcomes improved.** Meals began to taste better because they were prepared by hands that felt acknowledged; community cohesion rose because gratitude invited reciprocity.

"Think of gratitude as sunlight on soil," Guruji said. "Seeds of goodwill may already be planted, but many will not sprout until a beam touches them. Abhilasha's acknowledgement was that beam."

How conscious gratitude deepens and amplifies the effect

- **Notice the invisible first.** Gratitude that transforms is always aimed at what is unseen—effort, presence, small patience. Practice widening your attention so you can find those seeds.

- **Name the gift clearly.** 'Thank you for your hands' is more powerful than 'thanks'. Specificity hits the heart. It tells the other, *I saw exactly what you did.*

- **Share it publicly when appropriate.** Private thanks are intimate; public recognition broadcasts value and changes group norms.

- **Offer reciprocity, not expectation.** Help, return a favour, or create a small ritual of care. Gratitude that asks nothing in return still creates the conditions for mutual support.

- **Reflect on the ripple.** Later, journal or tell the group how the moment felt and what changed. Recounting embeds the lesson and trains eyes to notice next time.

Micro-practices you can use in the moment (two simple scripts)

- **The One-Line Shine (30 seconds):** Make eye contact, touch a palm lightly if appropriate, say one clear phrase: "I noticed how you did X — it mattered to me. Thank you."

- **The Two-Fold Return (2 minutes):** After you thank someone, do one small practical thing: clear their plate, fetch water, or offer a brief note the next day. That link between word and action locks the vibration deeper.

How to make the effect durable (turn small sparks into steady light)

- **Institutionalise tiny rituals.** A daily "kitchen pause" where one person thanks the cooks aloud; a communal jar for short notes of appreciation. Ritual makes the exceptional ordinary.
- **Practice 'gratitude audits' weekly.** Each week, a few people share one overlooked act and how it flowed outward; this keeps the community's attention tuned.
- **Teach specificity.** In group practice, model the exact language of thanks — it trains others to be precise rather than perfunctory.
- **Embody the feeling.** When you speak gratitude, slow down, breathe into the heart, soften the voice. The body carries the frequency; the more coherent the felt state, the deeper the field you broadcast.

When gratitude feels hard or forced

Guruji's gaze grew tender. "Sometimes the soil resists — pride, past hurts, or the false economy of comparison makes thanks feel like debt. In that case:

- Begin with *inner* noticing: silently name one small thing you did not expect and let your body feel that warmth for three breaths.

- Then offer recognition without drama: a quiet smile, a written note, or a practical return. Authenticity matters more than volume."

He added, "Forced praise rings hollow. Better to wait, feel, and then speak slowly from that feeling."

"Remember," Guruji said, "one spoken gratitude is like planting a sapling in a parched place. With patience it grows. With thoughtless neglect, it may wither. Your practice is the watering. The world you want to live in is partly created by the little lights you light each day."

He looked around the circle, and his voice dropped to a warm, intimate cadence: "Tonight, before sleep, write one small offering of thanks for someone whose work you barely saw today. Give it to them tomorrow. Watch the world bend toward care."

Practices to Elevate Your Vibration

"Energy," Guruji began, "is not something mystical that floats in the air—it is the language of your inner state. Every thought, every emotion, every breath sends a pulse into the unseen. Just as a musician tunes his instrument before a concert, your heart too must be tuned before it can create harmony with life."

He paused, letting the thought sink deep, then continued, "Tuning the heart is not achieved by force or will. It happens through small, consistent acts—moments that gather into coherence, like drops forming an ocean."

The Flute Maker

He told them a story.

"There was once a flute maker who lived by the river. Each morning, before touching the bamboo, he would sit quietly by the water, breathing with its rhythm. He believed that a flute could only sing truthfully if the maker's heart was in tune with silence. If his mind was disturbed, the flute would sound sharp or hollow; if his breath was hurried, the bamboo would crack.

Over the years, villagers noticed that his flutes carried a strange power. When people played them, the air seemed to soften; animals grew calm; even restless children fell silent. Someone once asked him, 'What is the secret behind your flutes?' The old man smiled and said, 'It's not the bamboo that sings—it's the peace I breathe into it.'"

Guruji looked at his students and said softly, "That is vibration. That is tuning the heart."

Simple Daily Practices – The Four Strings of Resonance

He then unfolded the daily practices as though revealing four strings of a veena that needed gentle tuning each day.

Mindful Breathing – The Breath as the First String

"Your breath is the bridge between the visible and the invisible," Guruji said. "Each time you breathe consciously, you reset your frequency. Imagine your breath as light entering your heart. Inhale peace, exhale resistance. Five minutes of mindful breathing each morning can dissolve the static of yesterday and awaken inner stillness. The breath aligns your rhythm with the rhythm of existence."

He paused, smiling. "Even one conscious breath can remind you that life still flows through you—that you are alive, and therefore, already blessed."

Journaling – The Second String of Reflection

"Write not to record your day, but to release its residue," he said. "When you pour your feelings onto paper, you lighten your energetic field. Gratitude journaling is not a list—it is a dialogue with your higher self. When you write, *'I am thankful for this morning light,'* you are training the mind to recognise abundance in simplicity.

Journaling clears emotional clutter the way rain washes dust off leaves. The more you write, the more your energy clears, until your thoughts begin to flow like a clean stream rather than a clogged canal."

Verbal Appreciation – The Third String of Connection

"Words carry frequency," Guruji said, his tone deepening. "When spoken with authenticity, they become waves that ripple outward, uplifting everyone they touch.

A simple 'thank you' said with presence can alter another's day—and your own vibration instantly rises. Remember, energy follows attention. When you recognise goodness, you amplify it. When you ignore it, it fades."

He leaned forward slightly. "Never underestimate the power of spoken gratitude—it is the music of the soul acknowledging its interdependence with the world."

Visualisation of Blessings – The Fourth String of Creation

"Close your eyes each night," he said, "and visualise every blessing you received that day—small or large. See them as golden lights circling your heart. This trains your subconscious to dwell in abundance rather than lack.

What you visualise with feeling becomes a magnetic current. You are not *imagining* blessings—you are aligning with the frequency where blessings already exist. Over time, this practice builds what I call a 'field of receptivity'—a stable vibration that naturally attracts harmony, synchronicity, and grace."

The Science Behind the Spirit

Guruji continued, his voice now a blend of wisdom and warmth.
"When your heart and mind enter coherence, your electromagnetic field stabilises. The body calms, the mind clears, and intuition strengthens. Just as a radio must be tuned precisely to catch a station's signal, your inner state must be tuned to receive the higher

broadcasts of life—love, creativity, and divine guidance. Gratitude is that tuning fork."

He lifted his hand gently, as though holding an invisible tuning fork. "When struck daily through these small practices, it vibrates through your being, reminding every cell that it is part of a greater harmony."

The Lighthouse and the Sea

"Imagine yourself as a lighthouse," he said. "When your inner flame is dim, the sea of circumstances feels dark and turbulent. But when you tend to your light—through breath, gratitude, reflection, and appreciation—the waves may still come, but they no longer drown you. Instead, they glitter in your illumination.

Your vibration is not about escaping life's storms; it's about shining steadily through them. Every act of gratitude polishes your lamp, every conscious breath fuels it, and every kind word sends its light further across the waters."

"Remember," he said softly, "raising your vibration is not a grand event—it is the quiet discipline of awareness. It is the small choice, made repeatedly, to turn your attention from what drains to what nourishes.

Gratitude is the tuning fork of the heart and mind. Strike it often, and you will find that even amidst noise, your inner melody remains pure. Over time, your presence itself will become a blessing—silent, radiant, and healing to all who draw near."

He closed his eyes for a moment, palms joined. "Tuning the heart," he whispered, "is not about changing who you are—it is about remembering the music that was always within you."

Tuning the Heart

Sam asked, "Guruji, what single daily practice could we wholeheartedly commit to that would raise our personal vibration and attune us more deeply to presence, clarity, and inner harmony?"

Guruji looked at Sam with a smile that seemed to hold the weight of centuries—gentle yet luminous, like sunlight filtering through ancient trees. A few devotees shifted slightly, sensing that the question Sam asked was not just his—it was every seeker's yearning condensed into one plea: *How can I live each day in tune with truth?*

Guruji closed his eyes for a brief moment, as if listening to something beyond sound. When he opened them, his gaze carried the stillness of deep water.

Guruji said, "The Practice of Presence – Listening to the Inner Current"

"There is one practice," Guruji began softly, "so simple that the restless mind often overlooks it. Yet it is the key that unlocks both peace and power—it is *the art of conscious presence.*

To be aware, even for a few moments each day, of the still current that flows beneath all doing—that is the single practice that attunes you to higher vibration."

He paused and drew a line on the floor with his finger, like a river winding through sand. "Your life," he said, "is like this stream. Every task, every thought, every emotion is a ripple on its surface. But beneath it, the water flows in quiet strength. To live in presence is to touch that undercurrent—to act without losing connection to the depth beneath."

The Weaver of Light

He then began a story, his tone deepening like dusk settling over a quiet village.

"There was once a weaver who lived at the edge of a mountain town. She made exquisite cloth, soft as a cloud and radiant as dawn. Yet her secret was not in the thread, nor in the loom—it was in her silence.

Before she began weaving each morning, she would sit with her eyes closed, listening to the rhythm of her breath and the hum of life around her—the rustle of trees, the songs of birds, the sound of her own heartbeat.

Only when she felt that still pulse align with her breath would she begin to weave. Each thread she placed carried that vibration of awareness. Her clothes were said to heal sorrow, calm anger, and even bring restful sleep to those wrapped in them."

Guruji smiled faintly. "One day, a young apprentice asked her, 'Master, how do your fabrics hold such peace?' The weaver replied, 'Because I do not weave with my hands—I weave with my awareness. My silence becomes the thread.'"

He looked around the hall. "So too must you live. Whether you speak, cook, write, walk, or work—do it with awareness. Let your silence be the unseen thread that weaves through your actions."

The River and the Reflection

Guruji then drew an analogy, his voice flowing like poetry.

"When a river runs clear, it reflects the sky perfectly. But when it is disturbed, even the sun becomes a broken shimmer. Your heart is that river. Presence stills it, allowing truth to reflect without distortion.

Every time you bring awareness to your breath, your heartbeat, or the moment before you speak—you are clarifying the water. You raise your vibration not by *doing* more, but by *being* more consciously alive."

The Pulse of Awareness

Guruji continued, his words becoming more intimate now, as if speaking to each devotee's heart individually.

"Each morning, before the world claims you," he said, "sit quietly—even for three minutes. Feel your breath without changing it. Feel your heart beating. Listen for that subtle hum of life within and around you.

That vibration—the one too gentle for the noisy mind to notice—is the same vibration that moves galaxies. When you touch it, you harmonise your being with the universal rhythm."

He looked toward Sam. "This is the simplest yet most transformative practice: to pause and listen—to be wholly where you are. Awareness is the doorway; gratitude is the fragrance that follows."

The Science and the Spirit

Guruji's voice softened into a tone of awe.

"When you enter this state," he said, "your heart's electromagnetic field becomes coherent. Science calls it resonance. Spirit calls it surrender. The heart and brain align, and the body becomes a vessel of harmony.

You begin to radiate energy that uplifts those around you—not through effort, but through your state of being."

He smiled gently. "The highest service you can offer the world is to live in harmony yourself. For when your vibration rises, it silently tunes others, like one string awakening another by resonance."

The Bell in the Temple

Guruji said, "In every ancient temple, a bell hangs. When struck with awareness, its sound does not end—it continues to vibrate through air, through stone, through silence itself.

You, too, are such a bell. Each moment of presence is like a conscious strike—its resonance moves through your life long after the moment has passed. A single day lived with awareness creates ripples that reach unseen shores."

He folded his hands and said softly, "Sam, if there is one daily practice to commit to—let it be *awareness itself.*

Be present to your breath, your words, your touch, your thoughts. Be present when you eat, when you walk, when you speak. Let gratitude be the fragrance of your awareness, not its demand.

When you live like this, you will not need to seek harmony—you *become* harmony. You will not chase vibration—you *embody* vibration.

For the universe sings most beautifully through the one who listens."

He closed his eyes for a moment, and the silence that followed was not empty—it was alive, humming with quiet truth. The devotees sat still, some with tears glistening in their eyes, feeling the invisible current of life moving gently within them.

And in that sacred stillness, they understood—presence itself was prayer.

"Let me narrate a story," Guruji said softly. His voice carried a warmth that seemed to dissolve the last traces of mental effort lingering in the hall.

The Gardener and the Seeds

"There was once a gardener," Guruji began, "who tended two fields side by side. Both had fertile soil, both were watered with the same care, both received the same sunlight. Yet, to his dismay, only one field flourished. The other grew sparse, its leaves dull and its fruits few."

"The gardener, puzzled and weary, began to grow resentful. 'Why does one field reward me while the other betrays me?' he thought. Every morning, he approached the struggling field with frustration—watering it not with love, but with a sense of burden. His hands moved, but his heart withheld."

"One day, an elder from the nearby village walked by. Seeing the gardener's furrowed brow, he asked, 'What troubles you, son?' The gardener explained his plight, showing the difference between the two fields. The elder listened quietly, his eyes kind and steady."

"The elder knelt, scooped a handful of soil from each field, and smiled. 'The soil is the same,' he said gently. 'What changes is not the earth, but the energy with which you touch it. In one field, your heart is open. In the other, it is closed. The seeds feel this.'"

"The gardener frowned, confused. 'Seeds feel?' he asked.

The elder nodded. 'Everything that lives responds to vibration. Gratitude is the sunlight that reaches beyond your eyes—it touches life itself. When you work with appreciation, you align with the rhythm of creation. When you work in resentment, you move against it.'"

Guruji paused, letting those words ripple through the silence. The devotees were motionless, their breaths almost synchronised with his.

The Shift Within

"So," Guruji continued, "the gardener took the elder's words to heart. The next morning, before tending to his fields, he sat quietly by the well. He placed his palms together and whispered his thanks—to the earth for its patience, to the rain for its gift, to the sun for its unwavering warmth.

Then, when he stepped into the struggling field, something subtle shifted. He no longer watered with anxiety; he watered with tenderness. He no longer weeded with frustration; he moved gently, humming as he worked. His work became prayer."

"As weeks passed, something extraordinary began to happen. The plants that once drooped began to rise. Their colours deepened, their fruits multiplied. The air around the field even seemed different—lighter, softer, more alive.

Soon, villagers noticed. They too began visiting the field to rest and talk. The garden had become more than a place of harvest—it had become a place of harmony. The gardener realised then that gratitude doesn't just grow plants—it grows peace."

Guruji leaned back slightly, his voice growing softer, more inward.

"The gardener's two fields exist within each of us," he said. "One is the field of fear and resistance, where we act out of duty, comparison, or expectation. The other is the field of grace—where we act with awareness and appreciation.

Both fields receive our effort, but only one receives our vibration of love."

He glanced around the hall. The devotees sat in deep hush, as though the air itself was listening.

"When we live without gratitude," he continued, "we may still achieve, but our achievements carry a subtle hollowness. They lack the fragrance of fulfilment. Gratitude does not change what we do—it changes *how* we do it. And that difference alters everything."

Guruji smiled faintly. "The elder was right: the soil is the same, but the sunlight changes the outcome. Gratitude is that sunlight—it warms what logic cannot reach."

The Frequency of the Heart

He lifted a small copper bowl from beside him and struck it gently with a wooden stick. The sound rang out—pure, expanding, lingering in the stillness.

"Listen carefully," he said. "This tone is clear because it vibrates in harmony. Gratitude creates the same resonance within your being. When your inner vibration is coherent—when your thoughts, feelings, and actions align with appreciation—life responds in kind.

The plants, people, and possibilities around you begin to flourish, not because the world has changed, but because *you have tuned yourself to life's music.*"

Guruji folded his hands and looked at his devotees with quiet compassion.

"So, my dear ones," he said, "tend your inner garden with love. Every thought is a seed. Every feeling is a drop of rain. Every act of awareness is sunlight. If you cultivate gratitude as the foundation, life will bloom in ways effort alone cannot achieve."

He paused, his voice lowering to a near whisper, "Gratitude is more than emotion—it is frequency. It does not demand that life be perfect; it allows life to *become* perfect through your perception.

When you live at that frequency, everything around you begins to grow—not by force, but by resonance. That is the secret of the gardener… and the secret of the universe."

The devotees remained seated long after Guruji fell silent. The morning air felt different now—lighter, alive, and luminous. Somewhere outside, the banyan leaves rustled softly, as though the earth itself had heard and smiled.

And in that silence, they understood: *gratitude is not something you feel after life gives—it is the vibration that allows life to give at all.*

EPILOGUE

The Lamp and the Mirror

"True prayer begins not with asking, but with thanking. Gratitude whispers what words cannot express — the soul's silent remembrance of wholeness."

– Shree Shambav.

Guruji, after a long, deliberate silence, rose from his asana. His robe flowed softly, like a subdued flame touched by the whisper of wind. The lamps flickered faintly, their light trembling upon the polished marble floor. He turned toward the gathered devotees, his presence serene yet grounded, his eyes glimmering with the quiet of one who had seen far beyond words.

"Let us conclude the day's session and retreat here," he said gently.

His voice carried a tone of both completion and continuation — like the final note of a raga that lingers long after the musician's hands have stilled.

He walked slowly toward the hall's exit, each step merging with the hush of the evening — a silence so deep that even the rustling leaves outside seemed to bow in reverence.

The Night Outside

Outside, the night had descended with gentle authority. The sky stretched endlessly overhead — a vast indigo expanse where soft, translucent clouds drifted across the silver light of a near-full moon. The banyan trees swayed lightly, their leaves shimmering in the faint wind. The air carried the scent of jasmine, sandalwood, and moist earth, a fragrance that seemed to calm the senses and stir the soul all at once.

From a distance came the faint rhythm of frogs croaking by the pond, the occasional chirp of a night bird, and the subtle hum of crickets weaving unseen patterns in the air. Fireflies began to emerge, their golden flickers dancing like forgotten prayers finding their way back into the dark.

The devotees stepped out of Buddha Hall, their footsteps slow, deliberate. The day's teachings had left their hearts full yet weightless — a feeling beyond comprehension, like still water holding the reflection of the moon. No one rushed, for the night itself felt sacred, as though it too was listening.

Their silence was not emptiness — it was fullness unspoken.

The Gathering

Eventually, they made their way to the dining area. The air inside was warm and fragrant — filled with the inviting aroma of ghee, curry leaves, and roasted spices. The clatter of ladles and the soft hum of conversation blended into a domestic symphony, grounding the vastness of the evening's silence into something earthly, nourishing, and intimate.

Each meal felt like an act of grace. Even the simplest of dishes — steaming rice, rasam, and coconut chutney — seemed infused with care. The devotees ate quietly, the earlier silence slowly giving way to gentle conversation. Words returned, not as noise, but as music — soft ripples upon the still pond of shared awareness.

When they finished, Akshaya, Padma, Vasudeva, Kiran, Vidyarthi, Aastha, and Abhirami walked together to the open courtyard. The air was cooler now; the wind carried whispers of the river nearby. They gathered around the fireplace, where flames leapt and crackled, sending small sparks spiralling into the dark.

The circle of faces glowed — illuminated not just by firelight, but by the unspoken warmth of connection. Their voices rose softly, reflecting on the day's session — the teachings of gratitude, resistance, and the unseen movements of the heart.

Before long, others joined them — Abhilasha, Akanksh, Akshatha, Apeksha, and Roopa, returning from a short stroll under the moonlight. Their arrival felt like a gentle wave washing onto a calm shore.

Padma adjusted her shawl and leaned closer to the fire. Around her, familiar faces appeared — Kieron, Astyn, Espen, Greta, and Divyani — each one carrying a distinct stillness, as though the wisdom of the day had quietly taken root within them.

Moments later, Sam, Alice, Sofia, Bhavya, Aarna, Dev, and John arrived, followed by Nita, Lalitha, Rohith, and Sujitha. The gathering had grown — a constellation of seekers encircling the fire beneath the open night.

Kieron, his voice low and thoughtful, broke the tranquil hum of the evening.

"Apeksha…" he said softly, "it has been a day of such depth. Would you share a story tonight?"

The fire crackled gently, sending an orange glow over the group. Apeksha inhaled deeply, feeling the crisp air fill her lungs. Her gaze lifted toward the night sky —

vast, star-filled, endless — and then returned to the circle of expectant faces.

She smiled faintly, a quiet knowing in her eyes, and began to speak.

The Lamp and the Mirror

"Long ago," she began, "in a quiet village nestled between two rivers, there lived an old woman named Amara. She was known for the radiant lamp that burned in her small home. Every evening, before sunset, she would light it—not merely to chase away darkness, but to offer light to life itself.

One day, a traveller arrived, weary from the road. He saw the glow of her lamp from afar and followed it to her door.

'Mother,' he said, 'your lamp burns brighter than any I have seen. What oil do you use?'

Amara smiled. 'I use the same oil as others,' she replied. 'But before I pour it, I whisper gratitude to the flame—to the hands that shaped this lamp, to the wind that allows it to breathe, and to the night that receives its light.'

The traveller frowned. 'Gratitude? How can a word make a flame brighter?'

Amara only gestured to a dusty mirror that hung nearby. 'See this mirror? When left unattended, it dulls, no matter how fine it once was. But when you wipe it clean with care, it reflects light perfectly. Gratitude is that wiping—it clears the dust that gathers on the soul. When the heart is polished, even a small flame can light the world.'

Days turned into weeks, and the traveller, curious, stayed on. He began helping Amara with her chores—fetching water, cleaning the courtyard, tending the little garden behind the house. At first, he did so out of obligation. But slowly, as he observed her quiet joy in each task—the way she paused to thank the sun before drawing water, the way she smiled at every blossom as if greeting a friend—something began to shift within him.

One evening, while lighting the lamp, he too whispered softly: *'Thank you, fire, for your warmth.'*

He felt a strange stillness in his chest—a warmth not from the lamp but from within himself. It was as if the flame and his heart had become one rhythm, one quiet beat.

The old woman noticed his change and said, 'Now you understand. Gratitude does not add to life; it reveals what was always there. It turns duty into devotion, repetition into rhythm, and light into life.'

When the traveller finally left the village, he carried no gift but the echo of that flame. Wherever he journeyed, people said his presence brought peace—like a lamp that burned without fuel.

He had become a mirror. He had become the light."

Apeksha paused. The fire crackled, and the night seemed to listen. Somewhere far away, an owl called softly, as if echoing the story's silence.

She looked around and continued in a quieter tone:

"Gratitude is that invisible flame within us. It doesn't demand, it doesn't strive—it simply shines. When we thank the ordinary, the extraordinary awakens. And when we see the divine even in small things, life begins to mirror that divinity back to us."

Her eyes reflected the glow of the fire as she added softly, almost to herself,

"Maybe that's what Guruji meant today—when he said gratitude is a frequency. It is not what we *do*; it's what we *become*. A vibration that harmonises with the whole. A song that the universe recognises."

The circle around the fire remained silent. Even the wind seemed to hold its breath.

Somewhere in that silence, hearts softened.

Someone felt tears they couldn't name.

Someone remembered a forgotten kindness.

And someone, perhaps, simply felt at peace for the first time in years.

The stars shimmered above like listening witnesses.

The night deepened into stillness.

That night, as each devotee walked back to their room, the fire's glow lingered in their hearts. The lamp, the mirror, the old woman, the traveller—they were all reflections of one truth:

Gratitude is not a practice to perform but a presence to return to.

It is the frequency of alignment—the light that never goes out.

Life Coach and Philanthropist

Shree Shambav is the visionary founder of the Shree Shambav Ayur Rakshita Foundation (www.shambav-ayurrakshita.org). He founded this institution with a lofty goal: to recognise human identity across gender, ethnicity, and nationality. Through this organisation, he wants to assist all communities in realising their full potential and the intrinsic beauty of life.

Shree Shambav, a Life Coach, is dedicated to supporting people on their journeys of self-discovery and empowerment. He assists people in discovering who they are, determining what inspires and drives them, and overcoming limiting ideas. His approach clarifies what one wants in life, assisting people through goal-setting and a step-by-step process for achieving them. He empowers people to make deliberate and responsible decisions, allowing them to identify their blind spots and evolve as individuals via the use of numerous strategies and tools.

The foundation's bold, uncompromising, and compassionate ventures are always aimed at initiating the "Inner Transformation" process. They focus on spiritual growth, personal growth, and self-healing while emphasising that true progress lies in "Inclusive Growth and Co-existence." This philosophy drives all their initiatives, encouraging a holistic approach to development and well-being.

Under Shree Shambav's leadership, the foundation has launched several impactful movements:

Shree Shambav Green Movement: This mission is to create a healthy, green, and clean earth through responsible water conservation and greening initiatives. The movement strives to make the world a green paradise by encouraging sustainable living and environmental responsibility.

Shree Shambav Vidya Vedhika (Vizhuthugal): This project aims to help students and children by offering training, books, stationery, and uniforms. It aims to provide the next generation with the tools and resources they need to excel both academically and personally.

Shree Shambav and his foundation exemplify the spirit of compassion, transformation, and inclusive growth via their work, which has a profound impact on individuals and communities around the world. His work exemplifies the power of acknowledging and nourishing the human spirit, creating a world in which everyone can reach their full potential and appreciate the beauty of life.

TESTIMONIALS

Journey of Soul - Karma - "We die in our twenties and are buried at eighty." Remember that nothing can stop someone who refuses to be stopped. "Most people do not fail; they simply give up." Shree Shambav deserves full credit. It allowed me to sit and consider what I might miss out on in life. The author has delved into every aspect of our daily lives. How can a seemingly insignificant change in these seemingly insignificant details bring us such joy? The Soul of Journey teaches you the "art of living" as well as the "art of dying."

Twenty + One Series - The rich cultural heritage offered a host in twenty + one short stories with incredible imagination, morals and values prevalent at a given time, influencing how people respond to a crisis or any situation. The author has recreated images with universal values and morals. The plentiful of fascinating from faraway lands would leave the modern play and story writers a cringe. The book supports trust and immeasurable values instilling hope for the new generations.

Death - "Shree Shambav's 'Death - Light of Life and the Shadow of Death' is an extraordinary masterpiece that delves deep into the profound questions surrounding our existence and mortality. The book's opening statement, 'Nothing ever truly dies; it simply ceases to exist in one form before resuming it in another,' sets the stage for a thought-provoking exploration of death's multifaceted nature. Shambav's remarkable ability to navigate the philosophical complexities of death and our universal fear of it is both enlightening and comforting. This book is a testament to the power of understanding and acceptance."

Whispers of Eternity - "Reading 'Whispers of Eternity' by Shree Shambav was a transformative experience that left me captivated from beginning to end. Each section of this exquisite collection delves into the myriad facets of existence, offering poignant reflections on life, death, and everything in between. Shree Shambav's verses are a testament to the beauty of language and the power of expression, inviting readers to embark on a journey of self-discovery and spiritual awakening. Whether celebrating life's simple joys or grappling with the complexities of human emotion, this book is a timeless companion that speaks to the heart and soul of every reader."

Life Changing Journey Series - "Life Changing Journey Series II Inspirational Quotes" is a remarkable collection that illuminates the path to self-discovery and personal growth. With its inspiring quotes and insightful reflections, this book serves as a beacon of light in a world often shrouded in darkness. Each quote offers wisdom, guidance, and encouragement, reminding readers of their inner strength and resilience. A must-read for anyone seeking inspiration and enlightenment.

Learn To Love Yourself – "A Heartfelt Guide to Authentic Self-Love." "Learn to Love Yourself" invites readers on a transformative journey to embrace their true essence in a world often focused on external validation. Through ten insightful chapters, it gently reveals principles of genuine self-love, guiding readers to deepen their connection with themselves. Beyond surface positivity, it encourages the cultivation of resilient self-acceptance, from embracing one's unique qualities to setting empowering boundaries. With inspiring stories and practical wisdom, this book is a trusted companion on the path to inner peace, fulfilment, and joy, helping readers build lives that reflect their authentic selves.

The Power of Letting Go – This book has been a gift to my spiritual journey. Shree Shambav's insights into attachment, personal growth cycles, and forgiveness are enlightening. The concept of seven-year cycles resonated with me, helping me understand the natural phases of life. I feel more empowered to let go of what no longer serves me and step into a life of freedom and fulfilment. A truly beautiful read!

A Journey of Lasting Peace – "A Journey of Lasting Peace" feels like a trusted friend guiding you through the maze of self-discovery. The 18 transformative principles are both practical and deeply resonant, addressing everything from gratitude practices to the art of letting go. Each chapter is infused with warmth and wisdom, making it easy to apply the concepts to my life. I particularly appreciated the emphasis on physical health's connection to mental well-being; it served as a wake-up call for me to prioritise my health. This book is an invaluable resource for anyone serious about personal growth!

Astrology Unveiled Series – "Profound, Logical, and Inspiring". What stands out in Astrology Unveiled is the author's dedication to making Vedic astrology logical and approachable. Each concept flows naturally into the next, backed by examples and exercises. The insights into karma and life cycles add a philosophical depth rarely seen in astrology books. Perfect for anyone seeking spiritual growth alongside astrological knowledge!

The Entitlement Trap - "Thought-Provoking and Challenging" The book challenges readers to confront their own sense of entitlement, and that's not easy—but it's essential. The Entitlement Trap doesn't offer a one-size-fits-all approach. Instead, it's a thoughtful, layered examination of how entitlement can limit our growth. The chapter on "Defining Your Own Hill" was particularly impactful, as it pushed me to reconsider which challenges are truly worth pursuing. A thought-provoking read for those willing to do the inner work to create a life they can be proud of.

Whispers of a Dying Soul – "A Soul-Stirring Reflection on Life's Unspoken Truths" **-** *Whispers of a Dying Soul: Unspoken Regrets and Unlived Dreams"* is a deeply moving exploration of the unexpressed emotions and unfulfilled aspirations that shape our lives in ways we often don't realise. This book invites readers to confront the powerful, often hidden impact of regret while guiding them through a journey of introspection and healing. Each page opens a space to reflect on the choices that define us—from moments of unspoken love to neglected passions—offering a gentle reminder to live authentically and courageously.

Whispers of the Soul: A Journey Through Haiku - is a mesmerising collection that speaks directly to the heart. Each haiku is a delicate brushstroke capturing life's fleeting beauty and timeless wisdom, inviting readers into moments of deep reflection and peace. This book is a balm for the soul, guiding us to find meaning in stillness and connection in simplicity. The themes of nature, love, and mindfulness echo universal truths, resonating with quiet, powerful grace. It's a book to be savoured slowly, cherished deeply, and returned to often. Truly, a gift for anyone seeking calm and clarity in life's chaos.

Whispers of Silence - Unlocking Inner Power through Stillness by Shree Shambav is a rare gem that beckons readers to pause, reflect, and reconnect with their inner selves. In a world that never stops talking, this book offers a profound exploration of silence—not as a void but as a rich and transformative space.

From the first page, Shree Shambav's writing resonates deeply, blending scientific insights with spiritual wisdom in a way that feels both universal and deeply personal. The author's ability to bridge the tangible and the transcendent makes this book an invaluable guide for anyone navigating the chaos of modern life.

The Power of Words: Transforming Speech, Transforming Lives - "The Power of Words is a profound and enlightening guide that has transformed the way I approach communication. Shree Shambav masterfully uncovers the hidden influence of our words on relationships, self-perception, and overall well-being. This book doesn't just teach you how to speak; it inspires mindful communication that fosters connection and trust. The insights on replacing negative patterns like gossip and judgment with kindness and authenticity are truly life-changing. The practical strategies and engaging narratives make it an invaluable resource for personal and professional growth. A must-read for anyone striving to communicate with intention, clarity, and compassion. Highly recommended!"

The Art of Intentional Living: Minimalism for a Life of Purpose - "The Art of Intentional Living is a refreshing guide to finding clarity in a cluttered world. With practical wisdom and profound insights, it inspires you to simplify, prioritise, and live with purpose. A must-read for anyone seeking balance and fulfilment."

Awakening the Infinite: The Power of Consciousness in Transforming Life - "Awakening the Infinite is a transformative guide that expands the mind and nourishes the soul. With profound insights and practical wisdom, this book beautifully explores the power of consciousness, helping readers connect with their true purpose and inner potential. It is a journey of self-discovery, healing, and spiritual awakening, offering clarity and inspiration at every turn. A must-read for anyone looking to live with greater awareness, meaning, and authenticity."

Beyond the Veil: A Journey Through Life After Death:

"This book touched me in ways few others have—it's not just about death, but about life, meaning, and the vast unknown that connects them. Beyond the Veil offers a graceful blend of science and spirit, inviting us to explore the mystery with awe rather than fear. The stories, insights, and reflections linger in your heart long after the final page. A truly transformative read that brings light on the shadows of mortality. It reminded me that in embracing death, we truly learn how to live."

Bonds Beyond Blood:

"A profoundly moving story that reminds us, family is not defined by blood, but by love, sacrifice, and the courage to heal. Every chapter touched my soul with its emotional truth and timeless wisdom. Through joy, grief, and redemption, this book captures the raw beauty of human connection. I saw reflections of my own family in its pages—both the pain and the hope. A powerful, unforgettable read that lingers long after the final word."

A Journey into Spiritual Maturity: 12 Golden Rules for Inner Transformation

"This book is a gentle yet powerful guide that awakened a deeper sense of purpose within me. Each golden rule felt like a mirror reflecting truths I needed to embrace. Shree Shambav's wisdom is timeless, poetic, and profoundly grounding. It's not just a read—it's a journey into the heart of who you truly are. A must-read for anyone seeking lasting peace, clarity, and inner transformation."

The Inner Battlefield: Overcoming the Enemies of the Mind and Soul:

"This book is a powerful revelation—an honest mirror to the battles we fight within. Every chapter is a step closer to clarity, peace, and emotional mastery. Shree Shambav brilliantly transforms ancient wisdom into practical guidance for modern souls. It awakened in me a new strength to face my fears and rise above inner turmoil. A must-read for anyone seeking true inner victory and lasting transformation."

The Seeker's Gold – Unlocking Life's Greatest Treasure

The Seeker's Gold is a soul-stirring masterpiece that goes far beyond the pursuit of wealth—it is a journey into the heart of what truly matters. Each chapter unfolds with poetic wisdom and emotional depth, revealing that life's real treasure is not found in riches but in the transformation of the self. As the protagonist evolves through trials, love, and profound realisations, so does the reader. This book is a mirror for every dreamer, a lantern for every seeker, and a companion for anyone walking the path of purpose. A timeless tale that stays with you long after the final page.

Born to Rise Series I & II:

Born to Rise – Series I & II is a profound awakening—a journey that begins in silence and leads you to the core of your true power.

Series I reshapes your understanding of success, showing that clarity is more valuable than applause, and authenticity more powerful than performance.

Series II takes you deeper, unlocking the mindset and inner strategy behind meaningful, lasting growth—not just in wealth, but in wisdom.

Together, these books are not just guides—they are soul mirrors, revealing the truths you've forgotten and the strength you've always held.

This is more than reading—it's remembering who you are, and rising with purpose, not pressure.

The Law of Attraction: A Soulful Path

The Law of Attraction: A Soulful Path is more than a guide—it's a spiritual companion. Shree Shambav has beautifully woven timeless wisdom with practical tools, helping me understand that manifestation isn't about control—it's about inner alignment and grace. Each rule in this book felt like a key unlocking something dormant within me. I've read many books on the Law of Attraction, but none touched my heart like this one. Through soulful rituals, deep reflection, and gentle encouragement, I began releasing old fears and stepping into clarity and peace. This book helped me move from desperation to trust, from wanting to becoming. It's a must-read for anyone yearning for meaning, healing, and true, lasting transformation.

Whispers of a Silent Monk

Whispers of a Silent Monk is a luminous blend of poetry, parable, and spiritual reflection. With rare grace and emotional depth, Shree Shambav invites us into a village transformed by silence, compassion, and timeless wisdom. Each chapter is a meditative journey into the heart's questions—of love, loss, identity, and liberation. This book doesn't just speak to the soul; it listens with it. A masterwork of gentle storytelling and profound insight, it reminds us that sometimes, the most powerful truths are whispered—not shouted. A must-read for seekers, dreamers, and those yearning for a deeper, quieter way of being.

"Mastering the Art of Gratitude:

A Journey from Acknowledgement to Awakening, Volume One" is a luminous guide for those seeking to transform gratitude from a mere emotion into a living state of awareness. Shree Shambav beautifully blends spiritual insight, psychological depth, and poetic reflection to awaken the reader's inner grace. This book reminds us that gratitude is not learned — it is remembered, rediscovered, and lived moment by moment, until appreciation becomes our natural rhythm of being.

The Power of Manifestation

"The Power of Manifestation is more than just a book—it's an awakening. Shree Shambav beautifully weaves ancient wisdom with modern science, offering not just theories but a practical guide for anyone yearning to turn their inner visions into lived reality. This book reminds us that manifestation is not wishful thinking, but a sacred, conscious collaboration with the universe. If you've ever felt the quiet ache for a life aligned with your heart's deepest desires—this book is your map."

ACKNOWLEDGEMENTS

To my grandfathers, grandmothers, mothers, fathers, aunts, uncles, neighbours, sisters, brothers, friends, and teachers, they poured in endless moral stories, retellings of Ramayana, Mahabharata, Puranas, Upanishads, and so on.

My teachers, neighbours, and kindred souls. Who provided us with a stage to perform wonderful Puranic stories and were gracious enough to acknowledge our efforts.

The artists and translators of epics have served as a source of inspiration, invigorating our spirits, making these works accessible, and enabling us to grasp the profound depths and deeper dimensions they contain.

I also cherish the stimulating conversations; I had with my wonderful mothers, Punitha Muniswamy and Uma Devi.

Our family's youngest member, Aadhya, who always overwhelmed me with questions, inspired this book.

I would likewise prefer to express gratitude to Mr Sivakumar, Mrs Roopa Sivakumar, Mr Akshaya

Rajesh, Ms Akshatha Rajesh, Ms Apeksha Prabhu, Mr Akanksh Prabhu, Mr Nikash Sarasambi, and Mrs Spoorthi Nikash for their valuable inputs.

I must thank Mr Rajesh, Mr Savan Prabhu, Mrs Revathi Rajesh, Mrs Rajani Sarasambi, and Mrs Manju Reshma, who encouraged me and often suggested writing a book. Their unwavering belief that I had something valuable to offer kept me going during my writing sessions.

Love you all,

Shree Shambav

Web: www.shambav.org

Email: shreeshambav@gmail.com

9 789356 350113

Printed at Repro India Ltd.